Big Tom

'One of the most charismatic and influential artists in Irish country music.'
President Michael D. Higgins

'A singer who brought joy and happiness to Irish people all over the world.'
Taoiseach Leo Varadkar

Big Tom

The King of
Irish Country

Tom Gilmore

THE O'BRIEN PRESS
DUBLIN

Dedicated to the memory of the late Big Tom McBride and Rose (King) McBride,

and to my own parents, the late Katie (Lally) Gilmore and William Gilmore.

First published 2018 by The O'Brien Press Ltd,
12 Terenure Road East, Rathgar, Dublin 6, D06 HD27, Ireland.
Tel: +353 1 4923333; Fax: +353 1 4922777
E-mail: books@obrien.ie. Website: www.obrien.ie
The O'Brien Press is a member of Publishing Ireland.

ISBN: 978-1-78849-064-1

8 7 6 5 4 3 2 1
22 21 20 19 18

Printed and bound in Poland by Białostockie Zakłady Graficzne S.A.
The paper in this book is produced using pulp from managed forests.

Photographs courtesy of the McBride family and Tom Gilmore, except the following:
Tony Gavin, INM: pages 41 and 226, picture section 2 page 7 (bottom); Steve Humphreys, INM: page 56; Dennis Heaney: pages 86, 87, 133 and 134, picture section 1 page 7 (top three); Glen Murphy: page 195; Martina Quirke-Daly, Galway: pic section 1 page 4 (top); Táine King: picture section 2 page 7 (top).

Thanks to PJ Cunningham for permission to use the extract from the book *From the Candy Store to the Galtymore*.

Published in

DUBLIN

UNESCO
City of Literature

Contents

Chapter 1

Born to Sing

From the land of Castleblayney, where the gentle rivers flow
To the shores of lovely Muckno, where the water lilies blow
With the grandeur of Hope Castle, so graceful on the strand
They bring me back fond memories of a noble Irish man
The Gentle Giant of Country, Big Tom it is his name
The idol of the starlight ball, from the drumlin lands he came ...

'Tribute to Big Tom', Des Boyle (singer/songwriter, Foxford, Mayo)

T om McBride was born to sing – and to be a king. But he wasn't born in a castle or a mansion – instead it was a humble whitewashed cottage, near Castleblayney, County Monaghan.

While his birthplace was less salubrious than that of an infant monarch, born in a chateau or a palace, Big Tom rose to become a monarch of the music scene in Ireland, and abroad.

But perhaps if a carpenter's son could rise from being born in a stable in Bethlehem to become the greatest king this world has known, why shouldn't the son of a Monaghan farmer, who wanted to be a carpenter, become The King of Irish Country?

In common with the Nazarene, who was crucified for what he preached, Big Tom was crucified for his songs by many of the music critics and some sections of the media. But he prevailed, and this would-be-carpenter from Castleblayney amassed a massive, loyal, loving legion of fans during his fifty-plus years as The King of Country in Ireland.

The only surviving sibling from the McBride family, Madge Kavanagh, who now lives in Birmingham, wasn't around for the momentous moment when her musical monarchical brother Tom was born. It was another four years before Madge entered this world, in the same whitewashed cottage near Castleblayney. But she has many happy childhood memories to share about growing up as the little sister of Big Tom.

Madge McBride doesn't remember the event at all, as her brother Tom was born four years before her, on 18 September 1936. Four children – Seamus, Tom, Madge and Willie John – were born into this humble rural home, to Samuel McBride, a Presbyterian, and his wife Mary Ellen, who was a Catholic. Madge has happy memories of growing up in a 'very happy home', in the drumlin lands of Monaghan, close to the Northern Ireland border.

Seamus, Tom's older brother, was another member of that happy household. He passed away twenty years ago, and Tom was deeply affected by his death – they were very close as brothers. On many days they mitched from school together.

The eldest of the children, Seamus emigrated to Birmingham, but some years later moved back to the whitewashed cottage at the Moy. He worked the farm and managed Tom's pub, The Old Log Cabin, for many years. Seamus passed away suddenly, while out checking on the stock on the farm.

Seamus's son Jerome plays guitar and sings in Declan Nerney's band. Seamus's daughter Deirdre has four boys, who are very talented singers and musicians – they are known as the Davis brothers. The eldest boy, Adam, plays the pipes, and he piped Tom's cortege from his home to the chapel on the morning of his funeral. The other boys sang the gospel song 'Some Day' in the chapel during the funeral Mass.

While the song 'Gentle Mother' launched Tom's music career professionally, it was his own gentle mother, Mary Ellen, who was the first to influence him into playing music and singing. In a 2011 interview with Pam Jackson in the Mount Wolsey Hotel in County Carlow, for Hugh O'Brien's 'Hot Country' television show, Tom said that he had been playing music since he was little more than a toddler.

'I was probably playing music since I was about two feet high, because my mother had an old radio and she would pick up stations such as Luxembourg and others that had any programmes with a leaning towards country music.

'She knew them all, and she could easily find them on the dial, and she would have the radio on for us all. Of course we would look forward to listening in, and I suppose my interest in country music started from that.'

Big Tom's gentle mother, Mary Ellen McBride.

Big Tom had great memories of also of another pleasant aspect of life in his home in the Moy, as he reminisced in an interview with RTÉ's Brian Carthy in the book *The A to Z of Country & Irish Stars*, back in 1991.

'One of my abiding childhood memories is of the Sunday mornings at home when we would have a feed of sausages, bacon and eggs, and it was something to look forward to all week long.'

His sister Madge has good memories of those Sunday morning and Sunday evenings too. 'When we were growing up, we would be up early every Sunday morning for ten o'clock Mass, and at that time you had to fast for three hours in order to receive holy communion. Then when we would get home, there would be the big fry-up of bacon and sausages and eggs,' recalls Madge.

'Very often also, when we would come home after watching Tom play in some football match, we would have a lovely bit of roast beef on Sunday evenings for dinner,' she says.

Tom's mother, Mary Ellen McBride, said she felt from when he was a child that Tom was going to be a singer. She said so in an interview with Donall Corvin for the magazine *Spotlight*, in the early years of his career. That was after 'Gentle Mother' and 'Flowers For Mama' had been hits. But she pointed out that those songs weren't about her.

Big Tom pictured with his mother, Mary Ellen McBride, in her home in the 1960s.

'Sure I'm still alive!' smiled Mrs McBride in the interview, conducted in 'her little whitewashed farmhouse, about three miles outside Castleblayney'.

'It lies in a leafy glade off a small winding road that is so out of the way you could never come across it by accident,' stated the interviewer. He added that while Tom was still a regular visitor to his parents' home, he now 'had a farm of his own', on the other side of the town.

'When he was young, he would always be singing around the house,' said his mother. She confirmed all those years ago what Big Tom often said since, about his mother avidly listening to the radio.

'I used to be listening to people singing on the radio, and I always knew that that was how Tom would turn out,' said Mrs McBride.

But Big Tom (then little Tom!) said he was less than successful with the first musical instrument that his mother bought for him.

'When I was a little older, my mother bought me a mandolin, but I never made a success of that. After that, I got an accordion and I played a bit on that. Anything I ever played or sang from an early age was country,' he told Pam in that television interview.

He has spoken in many interviews about how he bought his first guitar in London for £12. That started him off playing and singing before audiences, albeit initially in front of only a few other Irish emigrants, in flats around London, and later in Jersey (*see* Chapter 5).

Like many Irish people in those days, Tom went to work in the UK during his teenage years – in his case, in London and Scotland, and later Jersey in the Channel Islands. Tom told RTÉ's Donncha O'Dulaing in an interview in 1981 that the reason he left Castleblayney as a teenager and emigrated to the UK was because work was scarce in Ireland at that time, and the money was better over there.

'The money was a bit better over there. I remember earning as much as £15 per week, which was a lot of money at that time. I went to Jersey from London, where I did pipe-laying and picking tomatoes – you name it, I tried it,' laughed Tom.

Meanwhile, his older brother Seamus and younger sister Madge went to Birmingham, and Madge still lives there today. 'I went to England in the early 1960s, on the train from Castleblayney, and I have lived here in Birmingham ever since. When I moved there it was a big change, compared to life back home in Ireland.'

After decades as an exile in England, Madge still has crystal-clear memories of her older brother Tom, playing with her when they were children. 'There was about four years between us. My early memories of Tom were of when we played together in the yard and the fields, as well as going out farming and helping with the digging of the spuds or with the cutting and saving of the hay. There was plenty of space to play in the fields, and beside the river and streams too, and our parents would run us outside the house to play,' laughs Madge.

Along the winding leafy lanes
Where in childhood we would play
With heartache and old memories
I sadly made my way

'Back to Castleblayney', Big Tom (written by Johnny McCauley)

But Madge McBride says that while her brother Tom loved playing around his home area in childhood days, the mere mention of school had a bad impact on him: 'He was never happy about going to school.'

'He absolutely hated school, but he loved music. I remember him playing the mouth organ from an early age, as he just idolised music,' she says.

The McBride's grew up in a townland called the Moy, not far from Castleblayney. His parents were involved in mixed farming, having cattle, hay, potatoes and grain crops. They also raised chickens from eggs, which were incubated in the 'deep litter' system, according to Madge. Tom continued this practice for years, using an incubator that he kept in the good sitting room of his house, much to Rose's annoyance!

Tom always had hens on the farm, and enlisted his oldest grandson Stephen to help collect the eggs. Stephen recalls that he had told his grandfather that it was difficult to find the eggs in the loose hay in the shed. One morning soon after, Stephen found a number of blue-coloured eggs in the hay. He ran into his grandmother, Rose, to show her his discovery, only to be met with a laugh as she washed the eggs under the tap and the blue

Tom with his father Samuel (left) and mother Mary Ellen (third from right), brother Seamus and his children and uncle Peter.

colour disappeared. Stephen remembers Rose saying, 'Your grandfather painted the eggs so you could find them!' Tom was always playing tricks, and having fun with the grandchildren.

Madge McBride says they were only in farming 'in a small way' when they were growing up, and they didn't have a tractor at the time. 'Tom and my eldest brother would be rushing home from school – if they went! – to see who would get there first to get a spin on the tractors owned by a neighbouring farming family, who were also McBride's.

'We walked the three miles to and from school. You would be very lucky if you had a bicycle, but we felt we were lucky enough to even have rubber-soled shoes for our journey. If you had a pair of bootees you were lucky, and you had to wash them on Saturday night and spruce them up for going to Mass on Sunday morning.

'We grew up in a house that was full of music. Our father was a great singer, as well as our mother – it was on both sides of the family. My mother would wait up late at night, listening to music on the radio. You could wake up at 2am and she would still have the radio on,' says Madge.

She says that Tom, and all her brothers, loved working on the farm and around the yard. Farm life had its dangers though, and one particular incident stands out in her mind. Madge was trying to help Tom as he dug a hole in the ground to insert a wooden stake, and it almost cost her a finger!

'He nearly took one of my fingers off with a crowbar during that incident. Every so often Tom would stop, and he would bend down to take out the clay and a stone or two out of the hole he was digging. But it was when I moved in to help that he nearly took my finger off, and I still have the marks to prove it,' she laughed.

Tom wasn't aware that Madge was jumping in to help remove the clay, and he brought down the crowbar on the hole in the ground with full force. She hadn't time to pull back her hand before it smashed into her finger!

'I had my hand in there at the wrong time, and as Tom didn't have time to change the direction of the crowbar, it was my finger that got the hit.

'My father bandaged it up with whatever sort of bandage was available in the house, as there was no such thing as calling a doctor in those days,' added Madge.

'I remember that incident like it happened only yesterday, as well as when Tom emigrated to England. Then, when our younger brother died, and I was the only one at home with my parents for a while, until Tom came home to help run the farm. It broke my mother's heart when my younger brother died,' says Madge.

'I had a brother who died young at home,' recalled Tom in an interview that we did in his home in Oram in 2004, published for the first time in this book. 'As he was the only son at home, that is why I had to come back home to Castleblayney from the Channel Islands to work on the family farm.'

Madge told me in an interview after Tom's death that at that time, when her younger brother Willie John died as a teenager, communications were poor between Ireland and the outside world. This was long before the era of mobile phones, and even landline phones weren't available in most of rural Ireland. The family had great difficulty contacting Tom in the Channel Islands.

It was only 'when a telegram was shoved under the door' of where he was staying in Jersey that Tom got the sad news of his younger brother's death. 'It still took me a number of weeks before I could get back home, and the funeral was over when I arrived back in Castleblayney,' he said.

'I had the job of making contact with Tom on behalf of my parents, to let him know the sad news and try to get him back. It was so hard to reach people abroad, mostly only by letter or telegram in those far-off times,' says Madge.

* * *

When she moved to Birmingham, Madge McBride never thought that some day she would be going to see her brother Tom and The Mainliners playing to thousands of people at the dances in England.

'The crowds were so big at times that you could hardly get into the dancehalls, and if you got in, you had to stand up all night, as all the seats would be taken up early. That was the situation anywhere around Birmingham that Tom and the band played. I would go to those dances, along with a lot of my friends from different parts of Ireland and some from England as well.'

Madge is now seventy-eight. Her other brother, Seamus, died almost twenty years ago, while the most famous of them all, Big Tom, passed away in April 2018.

'My mum and dad were still alive when Tom started recording,' says Madge. 'Mummy died in 'sixty-nine, and there was a big age gap between her and Dad, as he was eighty-two when he passed away in the early 'seventies.'

Big Tom was as happy – perhaps even happier – working in the fields at home in Castleblayney as he was performing under the spotlights or on television. While they had no tractor when they were growing up, Tom was 'obsessed with tractors' back then. He ensured that in later years he had plenty of tractors, including vintage tractors that he kept around the farm.

'I was born and raised with them,' he said. 'The work that was done in my early days of farming in Ireland was with those small tractors. I still have a few of them around the farm. Scrap is what Rose calls them, but they all still work, and I love them,' he added.

His friend and singing colleague Margo O'Donnell recalls a funny incident in recent times regarding those vintage tractors. Perhaps it took him back to driving a small tractor for the other McBride family, the farm next door to theirs.

'A few years ago, when I was visiting the McBride home and Rose and I were talking in the kitchen, Tom appeared at the back door and he indicated to me to listen to what he called "a beautiful sound".

Big Tom at the wheel for Tom McGurke's 'Last House' television show in 1976.

'"Come out here, Queen of Donegal," said Tom, and I went out to the back door with him, where I could hear a buzzing sound. I wasn't very aware of all the vintage tractors that he had at that time. He said, "Are you listening to that? Have you ever heard such a beautiful sound?" and I replied, "A sound of what?" He had all the vintage tractors ticking over, and he said, "That is the most beautiful sound, and it's nicer sometimes than any music." Then he made a joke about Rose looking after the tractors and he looking after the flowers in the front garden,' laughs Margo.

From an early age, listening to the radio programmes that his mother would have on in their Castleblayney home, Tom McBride became a fan of the songs of Hank Williams. Hank had passed away tragically at the age of twenty-eight, over a decade before Tom started to sing, but he still loved those lonesome lyrics penned by the Alabama singer and songwriter. Hank had recorded in Nashville, but his slightly left-of-centre country songs, and his eccentric behaviour, were seen by some in the country music hierarchy as unsuitable for Music City USA in the 1950s.

Big Tom finally got to Nashville many decades later, recording an album there in 1980. His childhood memories of growing up in Castleblayney and listening to those Hank Williams songs were still strong in his mind.

Those memories from Castleblayney in the 1950s also prompted Tom to suggest to Johnny McCauley that he might write a song about Hank Williams's influence on the changing country scene of the 1950s.

That ultimately became the track 'Country Music's Here To Stay', which was popular on Tom's *Blue Wings* album. As he sang those lines in a Nashville studio in 1980, he was probably passionately reminiscing about his childhood days. Those days, and late nights, listening to Hank Williams's songs coming through the static on an old Pye radio, from some American Forces Network (AFN) show or Radio Luxembourg, are echoed in the song.

He introduced a rhythm new
An off-beat kind of country blues
And someone named it rock 'n' roll
Soon after he had died.
Hank Williams is the name
We owe the credit or the blame
Whatever sympathises with your point of view.
But all the drifting cowboys know
Who first gave life to rock 'n' roll
The world forgot to thank him
Now the honour's overdue.

'Country Music's Here to Stay' (written by Johnny McCauley)

'It was an amazing song, mostly about Hank and the 'fifties – the era that I remembered so well, back home listening to the radio. It even mentioned Jimmie Rodgers in some of the other lines. He was the very first man on record that was regarded as singing country. However, he wouldn't have been as country back in the 1930s as Hank Williams was in the 'forties and 'fifties,' added Tom.

From the late 1940s, through the 1950s and into the 1960s, Tom McBride's interest in country music was developing. Much of that was due to those songs of Hank Williams and others that he heard on the 'foreign' radio stations that his mother would tune in to.

His father, Samuel, was also an influence musically. He would sing songs too, both at home and in church. 'Music was on both sides of my family.

My father would often sing a song or two at night time, when people would gather in our home. He would also sing in the church choir on Sundays.

'Cousins of ours, the McGuigans, had their own band. They played a lot around this area. I had other cousins that played music as well. So I didn't start the music in our family – it was there long before me,' said Tom in an interview with Louise Morrissey on Sky TV.

'Our house was a céilí house, and people would come to sing, play and dance. Some nights when the neighbours would come in, we would dance all night.

'We would be dancing around the floor with all sorts of boots and shoes. So the music was there always, and all I had to do was just listen to those songs and tunes. That's probably what got me interested in music first,' he said.

'Country music is very similar to the old traditional Irish music. Songs with lovely stories to them. Some of them might be sad, and as a country singer I always called myself a sad singer of sad songs.

'But that's the type of stuff that I loved, and it was good for us in the band down the years,' added Tom in the interview with Louise.

At that time in Ireland, when céilí dances in the kitchen were all the rage, the number of country songs that Radio Éireann (as RTÉ was known then) would be playing was miniscule. Céilí, and other forms of traditional Irish music and songs, would be the most popular types of home-grown music, featured on programmes such as the appropriately named 'Céilí House'. It was an era too of great change culturally in Ireland. The outdoor crossroads céilís and the house dances were slowly being replaced by dances in parish halls.

Back in 1949, ten years before he was to emigrate, and when Tom McBride was only a year away from finishing primary school, his hero

Hank Williams was touring American military bases in Germany. The tour also featured several other US country stars, such as Little Jimmy Dickens and Minnie Pearl. Perhaps it was then that the seeds of country started to grow, in the mind, and in the life, of the big-framed young Monaghan man.

'With his song "Lovesick Blues" alone, Hank practically destroyed those people in the military bases,' said Little Jimmy Dickens, speaking about that German tour. 'They screamed and hollered for him,' recalls Minnie Pearl. 'The women especially,' she added, in the book *Sing a Sad Song: The Life of Hank Williams* (Roger M Williams – Ballantine Books, 1970).

Mrs Mary Ellen McBride and her family were listening to, and maybe even singing along with, some of those Hank Williams songs on radio broadcasts from Germany. And in doing so, they were nurturing the future talent of their own star-in-waiting, Big Tom.

When he became a singing star, Tom included some of the sad songs of his early hero Hank with other songs to create The Mainliners' 'magic mix'. Not only did those songs entertain the teenagers of that era in rural Ireland, and the emigrants too, but the proceeds from many of those dances helped many community projects too.

In his 1976 interview with Big Tom for the 'Last House' programme on RTÉ television, Tom McGurk said that many a school, many a church or a parish hall extension – 'even many a graveyard' – was funded by the proceeds of a carnival marquee dance where Big Tom and the band played.

Chapter 2

Born to Play

Just as Big Tom was born to sing, all of the members of The Main-liners were born to play. They were singers too, and just like the teamwork in any good sports team, they played as a unit – all for one and one for all. Positional switches in the musical team didn't matter to them. Indeed, the original lead singer, Ginger (Jimmy) Morgan, graciously and gladly stepped aside to become the pop vocalist and bassist in the band when Big Tom's 'Gentle Mother' became their first hit song.

Ginger was sanguine back in 1967 when it was Tom's song that the fans wanted above his self-composed 'Thinking Of You', which was intended to be the promoted song on their debut disc. Over fifty years later, Ginger is still as jovial and as gracious as ever about how Tom's song, instead of his, created the lucky break for them all. He says there was never any animosity about Tom becoming the big star in the band. 'But I will tell you that when

The guitar that started it all: Tom strumming the guitar that he bought in London for £12.

I saw him getting so popular with his songs, I had to start trying to become a better bass player, in order to hold my place in the band.'

Laughing loudly about himself and drummer Ronnie Duffy being described as the first pop singers in the band in 1966, Ginger quipped, 'We still are, over half a century later.'

Musicians in Irish showbands weren't writing songs, like he had done, back in the mid-1960s. 'Back then there wasn't anybody selling guitars in Castleblayney either!' laughed Ginger. 'I think our lead guitarist Seamus McMahon got his first guitar from Paddy Cole, who was in The Capitol Showband at that time.' In the corner of the band's dressing room, his colleague Seamus nodded and added, 'Up to then I was playing a fiddle in The Mainliners.'

The unassuming Ginger concentrated on talking about his memories of Big Tom, rather than dwelling on his own undoubted, but largely forgotten, songwriting talent.

'My first, and abiding, memory of Tom from that time was when he came back from England to live at home here. Not alone had he a guitar, but he was also a brilliant chord player. Tom didn't have to learn it, as he was excellent on the guitar at that time. I can clearly remember him also singing "The Wabash Cannonball" and "Nobody's Child" at our rehearsals in McMahons' kitchen, and other similar songs that we had never heard before.

'Most of the bands around 'Blayney at that time were orchestras. There was the Maurice Lynch Orchestra, or The Regal Orchestra. There wasn't the type of music that we were starting to play. Perhaps it was a country 'n' pop replica of the Royal Showband sound,' added Ginger.

He also said that all the young musicians in The Mainliners became even more excited when Big Tom arrived one day with what looked like a real Rolls Royce of a guitar!

'Tom bought this beautiful guitar and a wee amplifier, and we all got word to come out to the country to see this. He had it set up, and he could play instrumentals on it such as "Ghost Riders In The Sky" and "Apache" and many others. But later on, when Seamus got more experience on the lead guitar, he took over and Tom started to play rhythm.'

I put it to Ginger that he wrote many other songs in the years following 'Thinking Of You'. 'I did a few on an album for John Glenn when he was lead singer with The Mainliners,' replied Ginger. 'But the only other one that I did was when I went out on my own with a band, a few years after Tom had gone off to front The Travellers.

'It was just to do something different that I left The Mainliners, shortly after John [Beattie] had also moved out of the band. I wrote a song called "Rock 'N' Roll Band", as I was thinking to myself that this was the way I was going to go with the new band. It got a lot of good reviews, and RTÉ had it on their playlist for a full week. It got a play every morning, and I got a good lot of work for the band from that. It done good, and a few other bands recorded it. But I never wrote any more songs after that, and I don't know why I didn't,' he added.

Drummer Ronnie Duffy started out by using two knives to hammer out a tune on a length of copper piping when he was growing up. Early rehearsals with The Mainliners weren't much more sophisticated, or so he says.

'Ginger had been the first drummer in The Mainliners. When he started to play the bass, I sat in behind the drums. We were going to a gig in Cremartin, about four miles from where we lived, and the other band members had me singing harmony parts and tipping away with my fingers on the back of a seat in the small car that we were travelling in, to help me get the right beat. Just imagine – we were doing that drum rehearsal on the seat of the car while going to the gig,' roared Ronnie.

The hall they were playing in in Cremartin was a strange venue too, and a far cry from the big ballrooms and concert halls The Mainliners played in later, as Ronnie explained:

'At the end of the night, as the band were the last to leave the hall, you were expected to close the door and put a big rock against it, so that no cattle or other animals would get into the hall, until the next band came to play there a fortnight later.

'The door opened out, and so it had to be closed in when we were leaving. That was the security – no locks, no bouncers, no chucker-outs, only a big rock to keep the ballroom door closed. It wasn't heavy rock music – just a heavy rock,' he laughed.

'Looking back on those days, people will often say that Big Tom and The Mainliners were a country music band, but, just as Tom said to you, we were more a dance band playing a variety of music, and that mix worked.' A highly respected drummer, Ronnie has also played at many major corporate events around Ireland with his brother-in-law, noted jazz musician and singer Paddy Cole.

While Big Tom was the supreme frontman of The Mainliners, it must also be noted that Henry McMahon was the supreme band leader. He was there from the start; he was the backbone that kept the band going after Big Tom left; and even after his replacement singer, John Glenn, departed, Henry kept The Mainliners' name alive. There were a number of other lead singers, including Tom Allen (later TR Dallas) and a young Monaghan lady named Jan, who was formerly Shelly of the Big Valley Showband. And when Big Tom re-joined The Mainliners, Henry was once again a driving force behind those reunion tours of the late 1990s and the noughties.

'Well, the first reunion in 1989 happened in a simple enough way. It was the fans that kept asking if they would ever hear Big Tom and The Mainliners live again, and all the band members were enthusiastic to get back together again too.

'I always said that while we were still alive, please God we would get together again. Then, when we got together in '89, it was a superb experience for the full team, who were all well and willing to tour at that time,' says Henry. The crowds were as big, indeed even bigger at some venues, on those reunion tours than when Big Tom and The Mainliners first hit the big time, over forty years earlier.

Henry plays down a popular story from the early days – that the band had had to travel in a bread van to a gig when their first vehicle broke down.

'Well, it was the gear that we had to transport in a bread van belonging to our manager John McCormick, and that only happened once ever. But the band members travelled

Tom's good friend Jim O'Neill in front of the 'rusty tin shed' where it all started.

in cars, and not in the back of a bread van, which was a rumour that was spread at that time,' says Henry with a smile.

'When we became The Mainliners, we went from being a céilí band to having Ginger and Ronnie for singing the pop songs. As we also brought in Cyril McKevitt on trombone, it was out of necessity that Big Tom and I had to learn to play two saxophones, as all the popular showbands of that time had strong brass sections. I got the tenor sax first, and then Tom got a baritone sax,' he added.

Henry's brother, Seamus McMahon, started out playing the fiddle in a céilí band as a teenager. He said that he returned to playing the fiddle again, 'but only for a little while', just before Big Tom and The Mainliners reformed for some of their final reunion gigs a few years ago.

'I went back to playing the fiddle in a two-piece act named Showbud, with another musician and singer – Robert Browne from Rockcorry. We played mostly for social dancing,' says Seamus.

But while many country guitarists have admired Seamus McMahon's style of playing, this quiet and unassuming musician is very self-effacing when asked how he developed his distinctive lead guitar sounds.

'That style of playing more or less just happened, and we stuck with it. It also blended in with what John Beattie was playing on the organ, and it worked well for us right from when we started out rehearsing in our parents' home, which was only about a mile from where Big Tom lived.

'It was great at the start, as we were all from around the same area, and it was great when all the same lads got back together again with Tom for the dance tours over the past decade or so. Sadly then, of course, Tom died, and that changed everything forever for us all. However, we were pleased when John Glenn, who sang with us in the past, was available again to front the band, for some more nostalgic shows that the fans were looking for after Tom had passed away,' concluded Seamus.

Seamus McMahon's unique style of guitar playing has been cited by many as 'one half' of the very different sound that The Mainliners had. The other half that helped create that sound was organist John Beattie.

John retired completely from touring almost four years ago. However, speaking from his home beside the sea in County Donegal, the ace organist is happy to share memories of the days and nights when he was a Mainliner.

'We always kept it simple, because that was the way we could do it. I always had limited ability, but I just attempted to play to the best of my ability. What really stood to us at the live gigs was the fact that we were the ones that also played on all the records, and we could create that same sound on stage,' was John's modest analysis of what became known as The Mainliners' magic beat.

'If you listen to the chimes on the original recording of "Gentle Mother", I was playing a board organ, and that distinctive tone was exactly how the organ had to sound on stage too. We all had to play the instruments together in the studio, and if one of us made a mistake, the whole lot would have to be done from the start again. Now various instruments can be dropped in anywhere in a song, due to digital technology,' added John.

His colleague in The Mainliners, drummer Ronnie Duffy, added that he would love to go back to those days when all the instruments and the vocalist were recorded together. 'I remember that there would be a microphone going into where I was playing in the drum booth. As I was using the same kit of drums that I might be playing on for the previous five or six nights, up and down the country, there might be a squeak in the drum pedal coming through the microphone in the studio. So I would have to carry a small can of Three-In-One oil with me, and squirt some of it on the pedal if it was squeaking in the studio, so that the squeak would not make it as an extra on the record.'

John Beattie said that Ronnie and Cyril had joined the band before him. He was the last member to join The Mainliners after John McCormick took over management of the band.

'I had been playing in bands such as the Maurice Lynch Band and Pat Campbell's band, and we had toured in England and Scotland before I did the audition to join The Mainliners. At the time, I was also doing a day job, as the pay in bands at that time was usually about thirty bob [£1.50] per night.

'Before I joined the band, I knew Tom and some of the other members. I used to meet Ginger Morgan when he would finish work in McElroy's factory on a Friday evening in a local pub. We would have two bottles of Guinness, and it cost one shilling and eight pence – that was ten pence a bottle,' said John. 'Ginger was to be the lead singer until we got on "The Showband Show" on RTÉ TV, which was in black and white at the time,' he added.

From then until Tom left the band to form The Travellers in 1975, the organ sound of John Beattie was a vital component of The Mainliners' music.

'If you made a mistake or played in a wrong key or something, you would fix it up as best you could, but Tom would never give out to you about the likes of that. However, there are lead singers in the present time and they would get rid of you as quickly as you could change your shirt. But Tom wasn't like that – he was a gentleman to work with.

'I stayed with The Mainliners for about six months after John Glynn became the lead singer, and then I moved on to do other things, but mostly not musically. Then, when we all got together again in 1987, it was a more modern scene for a keyboard player, but I got back into it. I was very keen to come back, and have many happy memories of the reunion tours,' concluded John.

When Mary Kennedy visited the Oram GAA club for the 'Nationwide' television special in 2017, she also spoke to some members of the original Mainliners at the clubhouse.

Drummer Ronnie Duffy told her that Tom was much more than just their lead singer. He was a multi-instrumentalist too, who could step into the breach and keep a beat when a drummer suddenly took ill!

'It was a gig we were doing down in Castleisland, County Kerry, and about two or three sets into the show, I called Henry [McMahon], the bandleader, and said that I didn't feel well. I would have to sit down, or perhaps lie down, for a while. Henry went over to Tom before the next set of songs and told him.

'Tom just took off the guitar and sat in on my seat behind the drums. He adjusted the microphone that I had for doing my vocal harmonies. I went into the dressing room and lay down on the floor for about fifteen minutes. Tom drummed away, sang his own songs, and sang the harmony parts on other songs that I would have been doing. All I could say was "well done Tom",' said Ronnie.

'I never thought this would happen. I thought all this was over thirty years ago, but he is still huge,' said singer and bass player Ginger Morgan.

'It was nice at the beginning as well, because we were all neighbours,' said Seamus McMahon. 'Even in the early days we had good fun, and we used to rehearse in our home place where we were reared, which was nice when you look back on it.'

His brother Henry added that while people talk about the long journeys to and from dances on bad roads, the band never complained at all about the travelling in those days. 'I can remember one Monday morning early, when we were coming home from Castlebar, and when we got to Ballybay, just out the road, there was a man heading into town on his bicycle, probably to start his week's work. I was going home to go to bed, and so I said to myself that I was happy where I was, and doing what we all loved doing.'

Tom's manager and a former musician himself, Kevin McCooey remarked that the singer was a fatherly figure to many of his fans.

'So many people saw something in Tom McBride that made him look like a dad to them. Of course he was a fabulous singer, recorded great songs and The Mainliners were a really unique band as well,' added Kevin.

Carl Laverty was the goalkeeper in the Oram team that Tom captained. Carl was also there at the formation of The Mainliners. As their first manager, along with Henry McMahon he secured the debut dance for the group at Oram's small galvanised-metal hall, referred to by Tom McGurk on his 1976 RTÉ programme as 'a rusty tin shed'.

'As secretary of the Oram football club at the time, we ran a dance every two weeks in the old hall. Tom and Seamus McMahon played with a band called the Blue Seven at that time, while Henry and another one of the boys played with another band.

'I suggested to Henry that they should all form one local band, and after that I got involved, and we set about getting equipment and extra members. And so it came to pass that The Mighty Mainliners were formed,' says Carl.

Tom McGurk says that around sixty people attended that first dance, an estimate that Carl disputes. 'There were more than that attending on the night. As we live along the border, some dancers would come on minibuses from Crossmaglen or Keady and other parts of Armagh, as well as from Monaghan. It was always a great place for crowds, and there would be more than that there – perhaps well over 100 or maybe 150,' says Carl.

'I got them bookings all over Monaghan, Louth and Cavan, but it was mostly in small halls or at dinner dances. When they started to take off well, we got a date in the bigger Embassy Ballroom in Castleblayney.

'The vibes were good, and they were playing at a teachers' dance in The Riverdale in Ballybay, which John McCormick happened to be at. He probably saw their potential, and started to manage them shortly after that,' says Carl.

In an interview with the Evening Press in 1970, Big Tom said that even after John McCormick took over managing the band, the fees they could command were still very small.

'It was still a tough struggle for recognition, and we were playing for about £9 a date. Then in 1966, we played our first Dublin engagement. Christy Gunn, the owner of the Ierne Ballroom, agreed to give us five Sunday nights, at £50 a date. The first night was great; everybody from County Monaghan living in Dublin seemed to be present,' said Tom.

Tom told me in our 2004 interview that it was John McCormick who came up with the idea of calling him by the same name as lead singer with the band as he was called when playing at midfield for his football club – Big Tom.

'He got the idea that it would be an easy name to remember, and that it was a catchy one as well, so that's how it happened,' said Tom.

Big Tom was a reluctant star in the early, formative days of his music career. This shyness is described in comments Big Tom made himself, in a story published in the Irish World newspaper in London shortly after his death on 28 April. In that interview, Tom said that it was the song 'Gentle Mother' that 'pushed' him out front. He wasn't too happy about that, and it took him a long time to get used to being in the spotlight.

'It used to get to me … you'd be travelling and you'd go into a café for something to eat, and you'd hear people saying, "That's Big Tom!" That used to get to me, but I got used to it.

'When you look at it, if people didn't know you, you wouldn't be there, and it was a small price to pay,' said Tom.

Back in Oram, long-time friend and neighbour Jim O'Neill describes Tom as a reluctant star, who was as happy with his tractors as he was on stage or on television.

'I got to know Tom first when he became the boyfriend of my next-door neighbour, Rosemary King. Ten or twelve of us children from around the village would watch TV in the King household, as they were the first to have a TV in our area. Tom would sometimes arrive to meet his girlfriend on his bicycle, and we would know he was there when the bicycle was left against the hedge.

Did the youngsters who were watching television make themselves scarce when Tom arrived to court Rose? 'No, but I remember that Tom and Rose would make themselves scarce,' laughs Jim.

Tom's brother-in-law Paddy King, who later spent many years as bass guitarist and pop singer in The Travellers, remembers when his sister Rosemary was going out with Big Tom, and when they got married. He also recalls the crowds of local children coming to their house to watch the television when he was growing up.

'Our house was always full in the evenings after we got the TV, and it was like a cinema. Before that we used to say the rosary, but once the television came in, the rosary went out the window,' laughs Paddy.

'I remember when Rose and Tom got married, and they came back to the house that evening. There was no big reception, but they had gone for a meal somewhere out the road before coming back to our house, where we had a bit of a party.'

Paddy also recalled that 'I was only a youngster when Tom would take me out fishing and shooting. Later on, we played golf together. Tom was good at everything. I remember him playing football at midfield, and he was a very clean player. He would never pull dirty on any opponent, yet he was big enough to do so if he wanted to – but that wasn't Tom's style.'

Paddy says that Tom was a talented musician too. He could play many instruments, and would stay at them 'until he had mastered them'.

'I remember him taking up playing a banjo at one time, and he stayed at it until he had mastered the tunes, inside a few hours. He could also play the drums and the bodhrán, as well as the sax and guitar of course.'

'Another early memory that I have of Tom,' says neighbour Jim O'Neill, 'is when I first heard him sing after he came home from England. I was at a variety concert in the local hall, and there was a play by the local Pioneer Total Abstinence Association (PTAA). A man named Jimmy Brennan virtually dragged Tom up onto the stage to sing.' Well-known local entertainers The McArdle Brothers, Tony and John, were also performing at that variety show.

'Tom was at the back of the hall, and they virtually had to pull him by the scruff of the neck up onto the stage to sing. He sang one or two songs, but the one I remember most was "The First Fall of Snow". Everyone in the hall was moved by Tom's performance that night. He had a new style of singing that people here weren't familiar with at that time. We weren't very familiar with country music back then.'

That was the same rusty galvanised shed – which still stands in the village today – where Big Tom and The Mainliners played their first professional gig. According to Tom McGurk on RTÉ's 'Last House' in 1976, the mice 'scampered' around the hay bales at the back of this tin shed, and the cows in the field outside 'scratched on the tin walls'.

According to the caretaker, Paddy McGeogh, in an interview on that television show, 'It was obvious that Big Tom and the few other local lads were quite nervous. Big Tom was probably the most nervous of the bunch of them, as he wasn't a forward sort of lad. They played some of those hillbilly songs.'

Tom's mother, Mary Ellen McBride, was there on that first night when he and the band played in 'the corrugated iron hall at Brayside, Oram'.

That's according to the interview she did with Donall Corvin for *Spotlight* magazine. It also states that 'Mrs McBride was there too, when Tom posed for his first publicity photographs in front of the white church, across the road. Rose and Tom McBride and Tom's mother Mary Ellen now rest side-by-side in the small, sloping cemetery in front of "the white church".'

Mrs McBride also said in the *Spotlight* interview that because of his success as a singer, they were missing Tom around the farm. 'The only thing about Tom being in the band is that he doesn't have time to bring in the hay now,' she said. And when asked if he was good at doing that, Mrs McBride replied that 'he was the best for miles around. All the neighbours would be after him to help them out too. We all miss him for that.'

His neighbour and friend Jim O'Neill recalls those early days of The Mainliners. 'As a small boy, myself and my sister would come down here at night and look in the back windows to see the band performing. There would always be a crowd of us youngsters, looking in through the back windows and listening to Tom and Ronnie Duffy and the boys playing.

'My other memories of Tom are regarding when he came back from England, and he was doing a lot of odd jobs on the farm and working with local builders. Tom and another local man put in a concrete street for us at home. Because we had heard him sing in the local hall, he was already a minor celebrity with us children,' says Jim.

Later on, when Tom was a big star, and when Jim and other members of his family and friends were going to dances, he said they were all very proud of the success of their local celebrity.

'I remember us standing at the sides of the hall, and being very proud of Tom and enjoying his music, as well as knowing the songs from listening to his records. Tom was very generous to all us neighbours. I remember him giving my sister Ann a little record player as a present for babysitting his children, and we played all of Tom's records on that for years and years.

'He was very generous in giving us records – not alone his own albums, but also others by American country singers that he had collected over the years. His generosity to many people knew no boundaries,' added Jim O'Neill.

Chapter 3

Schooldays Over

In the folk song 'Schooldays Over' by Ewan MacColl, a teenager is told that his schooldays are over, and it's time to be 'putting his pit boots on', and to go working down the coal mines. We are slightly paraphrasing the popular folk song about mining, by replacing the name 'John' with 'Tom'. And while Tom McBride wasn't putting on 'pit boots' as a teenager, he was pulling on wellingtons to start farming at fourteen years of age.

'My last day at school, which I left when I was fourteen, was the happiest day that I ever had at school,' said Tom in an interview with RTÉ's Brian Carthy in the book *The A to Z of Irish Country Stars*, published in 1991.

Big Tom didn't like going to school, and his late wife Rose often confirmed this. He mitched time and time again. On one of the many days when his dad went looking for him in class, he found that Tom had missed school to pick potatoes for a neighbouring farmer!

Tom's father, Samuel McBride, was a widower when he married Mary Ellen. During his first marriage, he had a family of a boy and a girl, Bertie and Etta. They were the older half-brother and half-sister of Tom and his three siblings.

The school in Oram that Big Tom attended (as little as possible), pointed out by his close friend Jim O'Neill.

Samuel's first wife took ill, and Mary Ellen came to their home to look after their two children. Then, when Samuel's first wife passed away, Samuel and Mary Ellen married. They had their four children – Seamus, Tom, Madge and Willie John. In an interview with Julie Boyd in *New Spotlight* magazine in 1970, Tom said that he couldn't 'recall much of his early years at all'.

'He began school at five, and had with him a brother and sister at the same time at the tiny Oram National School, where today he still practises with his band,' stated Julie.

Tom laughed, looking back on the many times he played truant when he should have been at school.

'I can remember that I didn't like school at all, and I did my fair share of mitching. I used to hide in the rocks and wait till the day's end, when I saw the children coming home. Then I would walk along the road with them to our house, just as if I'd been at school all day,' said Tom with a wry grin.

'This went on till my father discovered me in the rocks and hauled me back into class at twelve noon one day. I'll always remember getting eight slaps on each hand for my efforts.'

Tom said that his favourite subject in school was reading – up until his death, Tom was an avid reader, and always had a stack of books beside the bed.

His pal in class then was John Mooney. John later went on to manage the Old Log Cabin pub in Castleblayney for Tom for a number of years.

'At fourteen, I left and started work on tractors, something I always had an interest in. At fifteen, I ran away from home, but I didn't get very far! I stayed with an aunt who lived about half a mile away for two months, until I surrendered and went home,' he added in that *New Spotlight* interview.

Two Castleblayney musical heroes – jazz saxophonist Paddy Cole and country saxophonist Big Tom McBride.

Tom's singing started quietly, mostly only occasionally at family functions, towards the end of his school days. While he loved country 'n' Irish songs, one of his musical instruments, when he joined bands later on, was a jazzier saxophone. One of his great friends from schooldays growing up in Castleblayney was another saxophone player, who has made his career in the music scene, mostly in the jazz genre – Paddy Cole.

Paddy was a childhood friend of Big Tom, and has spoken about how quick-witted the big man was – even in his younger years.

One of his recollections is from a time when the song 'Gentle Mother' was slipping down the charts, after many weeks in the Top Twenty. Paddy met Tom while crossing a street in Castleblayney and, while he didn't want to mention it, he felt he had to ask how 'Gentle Mother' was doing.

'Mother has taken a gentle turn for the worse,' was all that Tom said, and they both laughed.

Day-to-day life in Castleblayney became different once Tom left his desk at the local national school behind. He started working on his parents' farm, and with other farmers and later with builders in his home area.

So, schooldays over, then teenage years of farm work over, Tom decided to emigrate, with a little encouragement from another pal of his.

'I suppose it must have been five years that I remained doing farm work, because I was nineteen when a pal and myself headed for Scotland. Actually, it was the friend who took the notion to go, and I fell in with the idea,' said Tom.

The two friends made across the water, and began to find work in the Highlands of Scotland. It was an area that Tom said he 'grew to like', but he didn't take to working in Glasgow as well.

'Glasgow was a place at that time that I couldn't take to at all. It was my first experience of big cities, and the taste didn't appeal.

'We worked in the Highlands, on a hydro-electric scheme, for four months. Then we tired of that, and went back home to Blayney,' he said.

But after about two months at home, the travel bug started to bite Tom again. This time, he sailed for England.

'We got fixed up with work in Walls' ice cream factory in London. There I remained for a year-and-a-half, working a night shift all the time. It was around that time that I started fiddling around with a guitar,' said Tom.

In common with many other young Irish lads and lasses who had emigrated to the British capital, Big Tom found a touch of home in the Irish ballrooms there.

'On my nights off I went to all the Irish halls. The Galty, Fulham, the lot, especially when there was an Irish band over,' he said.

For many young immigrant Irish in London, and elsewhere in the UK, in the 1950s and 1960s, the dance halls were their main source of recreation. 'A woman's income was often divided into rent money, food money and dance money,' states Ultan Cowley's book *The Men Who Built Britain*, published by Wolfhound Press in 2001.

According to Ultan Cowley's book, there was a dress code in some of the Irish ballrooms in the UK. 'The men dressed in navy blue suits, with a white shirt and a blue or red tie. In the Gresham Ballroom, London, as elsewhere, a tie could be rented for a shilling (twelve old pence) at the door prior to admission.

'The women wore ballroom dresses, or in the 1960s, skirts with three-tier stiffened petticoats underneath to make them stand out from their bodies,' states Ultan Cowley in his book, which is subtitled 'A History of the Irish Navvy'.

But while finding out where the Irish ballrooms were located in London seemed to be no problem for Tom and his friends, it seems that accommodation was far more difficult to come by.

'Funnily enough, one of my most vivid memories of London when I arrived was the shortage of accommodation. At that time it was almost impossible to get digs,' he said to me in our 2004 interview.

Even after Tom and the lad that he was sharing digs with finally got sorted out, a mini-disaster was to see them literally thrown out on the streets of London again.

'The other lad left the tap on by mistake one night. Naturally enough, by the following morning the water had seeped through the floorboards to the kitchen below, and we were given twenty-four hours to get out. I'll never forget that, knowing the hard slog that we would have ahead again, just to get new digs.'

He added that, just like Glasgow, he never really liked the big city of London. 'Over there, everybody seemed to be rushing around, and after a while I was rushing around like the worst of them,' he laughed.

But he realised that 'when that was happening', it was 'time to take stock' of himself.

'I just wondered what all this rushing around was for, and decided to slow down, as much as I could. After a year-and-a-half, my pal and I headed off to the Channel Islands.'

They travelled to Jersey, where Tom and his friend worked at picking tomatoes, and then worked on the buildings for another year-and-a-half.

'I liked it there, and there was a country band in Jersey who called themselves The Mainliners,' added Tom. Elsewhere in this book, in the 2004 interview that I did with Tom, he said that he 'swiped' that name, and years later used it for the band that he was to famously front.

That was the dancing scene that young Tom McBride was to experience as a teenager, after he finished his primary school education at fourteen, but it was to change, albeit slowly, as Ireland changed culturally and socially in the 1960s.

Big Tom and The Mainliners, Philomena Begley and her band and many others were instrumental (pardon the pun!) in that cultural change. They moved away from playing céilí music and started playing country during that decade, but the scene at the dances – where girls met boys or, if you prefer, boys met girls – still remained similar to previous times.

'In fact, the men would stay on one side of the hall and the women on the other, and the priests would patrol the place, making sure that no one got too close or personal!' recalls Philomena Begley in her book *Philomena Begley: My Life, My Music, My Memories* (O'Brien Press).

Big Tom's memories are very similar and equally humorous. 'If you were brave enough to make it across the floor, and you didn't get the one you wanted, then you'd need to want the one that you got,' was one of his favourite sayings.

Some of the song played at the dances and recorded by Big Tom and The Mainliners during those early days also were songs recorded by Hank Williams and a man who is credited with being one of the first country singers to record – Jimmie Rodgers, who was another early country music influence on Big Tom.

A theme these singers shared was songs about railways, and several Jimmie Rodgers train songs were recorded by Big Tom, as well as new Irish ones. An example is Big Tom's song, co-written with Henry McMahon, 'The GNR Steam Train'. Back in the early 1930s, Jimmie Rodgers was singing about 'Waiting For A Train'. Both of these songs evoke the loneliness of travelling far from home. The late Boxcar Willie was another singer of train songs, songs that Tom also loved:

The songs of Boxcar Willie
They take me back again
To my childhood days in 'Blayney
When I saw my first steam train.
Now the first time that I rode that train
Oh! How my poor heart felt
I was just another emigrant
On my way to Hollyhead.
I was leaving home that morning
To seek fortune and fame

So I left Castleblayney
On the GNR steam train.
She took many folk away from home
And brought them back again.

'The GNR Steam Train' (Henry McMahon/Tom McBride)

As a line in the song 'The GNR Steam Train' states, Tom was one of those that was brought back home again … on the 'GNR Steam Train'.

Henry McMahon of The Mainliners explains how that song came to be written, with a little help from his colleague in the band Big Tom.

'I was sitting in the car one day when a selection of train songs by Boxcar Willie came on the radio. I suddenly thought that there were very few Irish train songs, apart from the Percy French one ['Are Ye Right There Michael', a song about the West Clare Railway].

'So I sat down and we wrote 'The GNR Steam Train', which was simple enough to do, because it was a history of the train that went from Castle-blayney when we were growing up.'

In an interview with the *Sunday World* newspaper in the early 1970s, Big Tom talked about how many American train songs may have had Irish roots.

'Country music started off on the railroads, where fellows would be making up songs about home. And probably it would follow that many of those same people were Irish,' said Big Tom.

In the same interview, he explained that country music is sentimental 'the whole world over'. Tom's biggest hit in the latter years of his career was 'Going Out The Same Way You Came In', while Hank Williams's last release before his untimely death on New Year's Day 1953 was 'I'll Never Get Out Of This World Alive' – interesting parallels.

Tragically, Hank, then known as 'The King of Country Music', was found dead in the back of a car on the way to a gig in Canton, Ohio, at twenty-nine years old. But his songs lived on, and still live on today. Decades after Hank's death, when Big Tom became known as 'The King of Irish Country', he was reviving and recording some of the Hank Williams songs that he first heard on radio as a boy.

During Tom's boyhood, the fair days, when livestock were sold on the streets of most rural towns, were big occasions. Big Tom recalled some of his memories from those fair days of his childhood and teenage years, in an interview with Border Region TV in 2015.

'Cattle and sheep, horses, pigs and turkeys would be bought and sold during the fair days back then.

'In the olden days, the men would be buying and selling on the streets, there would be hands clapping when a deal was done. There would be an odd drink or two in between the dealing. But you could also get a black eye at some of those fair days,' he laughed.

When asked if he was ever involved in such unruly behaviour, Big Tom replied, 'I was too young then to get involved in any of that sort of activity.'

But it was a time of tremendous change – not just in the little villages around Castleblayney, but around the world, as countries recovered from the Second World War. The world of country music was changing too. If Hank Williams, during his all-too-brief career, was introducing blues influences into country, it was only a blip on the radar in 1950. Hank's music was only a precursor to the massive musical changes that were soon emanating from Sun Studios in Memphis, Tennessee. Former country singer Elvis Presley spearheaded a musical revolution that Hank Williams might have been a major part of if he had lived. That Memphis musical revolution resulted in much of country morphing into the new sound called rock 'n' roll in the mid-1950s.

Socially, culturally, and in practical ways too, rural Ireland was changing, even if rock 'n' roll was slower to arrive here. Donegal ballad singer Bridie Gallagher, and another Ulster singer, Ruby Murray, were Ireland's international recording stars then. A little later, Tom Dunphy would have the first country 'n' Irish hit single – 'Katie Daly', with 'I Heard The Bluebirds Sing' on the B-side.

About this time, the showbands were emerging: The Clipper Carlton, The Royal, The Capitol, The Drifters, The Johnny Flynn Showband, The Dixies and many more. But Big Tom and The Mainliners had not yet appeared on the scene. Even though his schooldays were now long over, Tom McBride had not yet donned a showband suit. Football, and not music, was still his main pastime. That's according to journalist and broadcaster Patsy McCardle, writing in the *Top Rank Entertainment News* magazine years later.

'On Sundays and during the long summer evenings, as the mists reluctantly dropped over lovely Lough Muckno, Tom would be found booting a football "with the lads". That was in the low lying meadows, not far from his snug little County Monaghan farmhouse home, near the border town of Castleblayney,' states the story.

Tom's former football colleague Carl Laverty says: 'He put Oram on the map, both in terms of football and music, during the early to mid-1960s.'

Cars were still rare enough on rural roads at that time. Usually the only people who had them were the doctor, the priest and the vet. Television sets were similarly rare in rural villages in the early 1960s. Farms were creaking slowly towards some semblance of mechanisation and modernisation.

The move was on to change from the old ways of working with horses and ploughs, or with the ass and cart. Those years heralded the arrival in Irish farms of the small tractors that Big Tom grew to love almost as much as his music!

Tom was brought up on just such a small farm, in those changing times, about fifteen miles from the home of the famous Irish poet Patrick Kavanagh in Inniskeen.

'He had never met poet Kavanagh – although he knew all about *Tarry Flynn*, one of the books that made Paddy Kavanagh famous,' according to a story on Tom written by Gus Smith in the *Sunday Independent* in the late 1960s.

Another man from Inniskeen, who became a close friend of both Tom and Rose McBride, is businessman John Pepper. He says that those who emigrated before, during and after Big Tom's time as an exile in England all identified with his songs.

'He highlighted the curse of enforced emigration from our nation, the painful void it created and the legacy of loss that continues within the Irish psyche.

'Big Tom could identify with this from his time as an emigrant himself. It is no wonder that Big Tom and The Mainliners remained such big crowd-pullers wherever they played throughout England,' says John.

'For those of us who never had to emigrate, or stand on a stranger's floor, Big Tom gave us "The GNR Steam Train" and "They Covered Up The Old Swimming Hole" as reminiscent reminders of days long past.

'Big Tom touched the hearts of thousands of emigrants through the vivid pictures he painted, in "Back To Castleblayney", "5000 Miles From Sligo", "Isle Of Innisfree", "Ghost Of Glengevlin", "I'll Settle For Old Ireland", "My Old Home In Mayo", "An Irish Nurse", "I Have An Aged Mother"; not forgetting his big hit, "Four Country Roads",' says John.

Tom started out doing some farming in the tiny fields and little hills of his home area of Monaghan during his youth, and he never lost that love of the land. Even with all the music success that he enjoyed over the years, he also did 'a wee bit of farming' in tandem with his showbusiness career.

However, when I interviewed him to 2004, he said the farming for him was very different in the 1950s, when he started out in the fields.

'I still do a little bit of farming – about thirty yards by twenty in the garden! Dermot, a son of mine, does the farming now; he looks after the cattle and all that sort of stuff. I retired from running around the hills after cows and heifers and bulls a while ago,' said Tom with a wry grin. It was a typically witty reply regarding his 'retirement'.

Suddenly for this red-haired youngster, school days in Oram were over. But reminiscing about those times over the years, Big Tom would smile and say that school days 'were never on' for him anyway!

Chapter 4

A Football Star
and All-Round
Sportsman

F ootball was big for Big Tom when he was growing up, as it was also for another Monaghan bard, Patrick Kavanagh, one of Ireland's greatest poets. Gaelic football remained big for Big Tom all his life, and continues to be big for his children and grandchildren today. But Tom was an all-round sportsman. He also played golf, was a keen fisherman, had a speedboat on Lough Muckno and loved to play snooker. He had a full-size snooker table installed at his home, and spent many an evening playing with family and friends into the wee small hours.

When they were growing up, that snooker table was also a big attraction for Tom's sons, Thomas Junior and Dermot. Their pals arrived at their home to play snooker so regularly that sometimes it seemed like a youth club for the whole area as well!

It was his football teammates who named him Big Tom when, as a majestic midfielder, he captained the Oram GAA team to win the County Monaghan Junior Championship and League in 1963. It was a memorable time for the little rural club, as Carl Laverty, who played beside Tom on that team, recalls.

'We played together on the Oram football team for years and, as time went by, both Tom and Rose were very involved in the development of the Oram Community Centre. Even when Tom would be away touring, Rose would still be on the phone to me two or three times a week regarding the development of that centre,' says Carl.

Carl lives just out the road from Oram, on the route to Keady, County Armagh, and he remained one of the best friends of Tom and Rose McBride over the decades. He also says he was the first manager of The Mainliners, as he booked some of the first ever dance dates for them. Carl says that the generosity of the McBrides to their local GAA club, and to many other charitable causes, knew no bounds.

I was born in Mullyash, which is further up towards the border, but we all trained together in a local area called The Meadows,' said Carl. 'Tom was vital for us in the middle of the field. I could often watch from the goals as the high-fielding centre-field duels were taking place.

'I have been friends with Tom since I played in goal on the 1963 Oram team that he captained to win the county junior double. I can still remember the big giant in the middle of the field. He was a giant, and was gentle when the going was loose. But football was rough and tough at that time, and when something had to be sorted out, Tom would be quickly in there too, and it would be sorted.'

Over the years, Carl and Tom remained firm friends. Carl operates the Car-L motor parts company in Dundalk, but his love of football means that much of his spare time is taken up as Chairman, Secretary, Treasurer, and in almost every other

Big Tom, King of Monaghan Junior Football, 1963.

backroom duty with his local football club. Over the decades, he has always been involved in fundraising for the Oram football club, and Big Tom not alone played on the field for Oram, but has always played a massive part in raising money for the club as well.

'Any fundraiser that we needed for any organisation locally, we could call on Tom and Rose to help. Not alone was he a loyal captain for our team back in 1963, but decades later, when we developed the club and community centre, at a cost of £800,000, Big Tom played more dates free of charge for us than we could ever remember,' said Carl.

It was in that community centre that Big Tom's body was laid out. Thousands of people, local and from further afield, filed past his coffin there following his passing. Carl Laverty says it was only right and fitting that the local club should facilitate that farewell to one of its most loyal servants.

'A lot of people rang us and sent letters of praise for what we did regarding the Guard of Honour, and how our GAA club rose to the occasion.

But my God, if we couldn't do it for Tom, we would have done it for nobody, as he did so much for all of us,' added Carl.

Success on the football playing fields of Ireland was short-lived for Tom McBride, as his success as a singer started to mushroom. He had to leave behind the playing fields of Oram and Monaghan for playing of a different sort – in the ballrooms of Ireland and the UK. There were other fields too – ones that temporarily housed marquees, where many of his dances helped raise funds for other GAA playing fields all around the country.

But the locals around Oram and Castleblayney, especially the older people, remain loud in their praise for Big Tom as a footballer of note in his younger days. However, when I mentioned it to him, Tom gave me one of his typical self-effacing replies.

'I played football badly, but I did play for the county team once or twice, and for the local team as well. But that was around the time that the band had started to go well, and so I had to make a decision if it was going to be football or music. I went with the music, and I would probably never have made it anyway as a great footballer. You could say that I was there or thereabouts,' he laughed.

It was on the football field too that he first got the name Big Tom, because he was such a lanky midfield player. There was also a famous Cavan footballer named Tom O'Reilly who was known as Big Tom. So the footballer friends of Tom McBride named him likewise. Later, when local dance promoter John McCormick started to manage The Mainliners, he decided that Big Tom was an ideal stage moniker for the big fellow who was the band's lead singer.

'The name was easy to remember; everyone seemed to like it, and it stuck to me from then on,' said Tom.

The next footballing generation: Thomas Junior and Dermot McBride in their Oram club jerseys.

He loyally supported his local club in Oram and his native Monaghan all his life, and followed their fortunes closely. His children and grandchildren also play the game, with his son Dermot still helps to train local teams in Oram. Whenever he could, Tom travelled to games that Monaghan played in all over Ireland, and even if the county team had lots of disappointments, he never faltered in his fulsome support for the teams.

'We always have high hopes for Monaghan,' said Tom with pride about his favourite sport and his favourite county as he gazed out on what he called 'the little hills of Monaghan' from the window of his home.

He was a great supporter of Mayo football too, according to his long-time friend, songwriter, journalist, broadcaster and television presenter Michael Commins. Tom and Michael would often talk on the phone about matches that both Monaghan and Mayo should, and possibly could, have won. But as the old Irish adage states, 'they didn't have the rub of the green' in so many finals. But Michael says that 'after Monaghan, Mayo was his favourite football team'.

The plaque erected by the people of Oram in 2005 in honour of Big Tom, 'in recognition of the great musical entertainment, memories and happiness he has brought'.

'He supported his home GAA club of Oram and Monaghan with a passion, the blue-and-white flag of Monaghan flying proudly in the garden of his home. In his early twenties, Tom donned the county jersey on a number of occasions too,' stated Michael in a tribute page in the *Mayo News*, on 24 April 2018.

'Tom had a great fondness for Mayo and the West of Ireland in general because of all the emigrants from this area that he met in England. He was as heartbroken as we were in the last few years when Mayo lost All-Ireland finals by a point. Rose always rang me before I went and when I was coming back from those matches,' said Michael in a separate interview with Mid-West Radio on the day that Tom passed away.

While there is intense football rivalry between many neighbouring counties in Ireland, and there is no love lost on the football fields when teams from Monaghan and Tyrone or Galway and Mayo meet, the love of the music of Big Tom often resulted in romantic love affairs blossoming between fans from rival football counties!

One such example is the love between Julie Conway, from Killawalla in Mayo, and Michael Donnellan, from Tuam in Galway. Despite being staunch supporters of rival football teams, the two fell in love at a Big Tom dance, and subsequently married. They are just one example of many couples who met at Big Tom dances down through the decades.

Long before Julie, who is a talented artist, mostly in oils, ever met Michael, she was a fan of Big Tom. She began listening to his music when she was in fifth class at Sraheen National School in Killawalla, near Westport, County Mayo. Julie once hitched all the way from Donegal to Cork to attend two Big Tom dances on successive nights.

'Myself and my sister and a friend of ours from Castlebar hitched all the way down from Raphoe in Donegal to Cork when we were in our early twenties. We stayed in a B&B in Cork, and hitched back again the next day,' says Julie.

'You could hitch to a dance that time, and you could nearly hitch home afterwards, because it seemed safe to do so,' she added.

Her husband of over thirty years, Michael Donnellan from Tuam in County Galway, said that even after three decades together, they both still support different football teams. 'She still shouts for Mayo, while I'm a Galway fan of course. But sport didn't matter, as we are both life-long fans of Big Tom.'

Love blossomed for the two country music and sports fans from the moment they met at a Big Tom dance in Cong, County Mayo. A week later, they got together again at a dance in Glenamaddy, and it was love for life after that – apart from occasional squabbles about football!

Lovers and lovers of Big Tom but football rivals Michael and Julie Donnellan from Tuam.

'We travelled everywhere to see Big Tom – to Wexford, Cork, Kerry, Northern Ireland, often two or three nights in a row. During his 2012 comeback tour, we went to seventeen out of the eighteen dances that he did. We would have gone the eighteenth night too, but we were in Spain on holidays,' said Michael.

Julie has a bulging scrapbook of press cuttings, autographed photographs, calendars and all manner of memorabilia that she has carefully collected since her primary school days. She and Michael became such great friends with Tom and Rose that 'The King of Irish Country' came to Tuam to open an extension to their Town and Country garage, filling station and motor factors in 1997.

'We are together in loving the songs of Tom, but we are not together at all when our two rival counties play football – even after all these years,' laughed Julie.

The interest in football that Tom had, be it Monaghan, Mayo or many other counties too, was also confirmed for this book by his long-time friend and fan PJ Granaghan from north Mayo, and by Tom's long-time manager and former bandmate Kevin McCooey.

With a laugh, PJ said that while Tom had an interest in Mayo football, it was 'Monaghan that came first anyway'.

'He never missed many matches in Clones, and as I often stayed over on a Saturday night in their home with Rose and Tom, the dinner would always be early on Sunday, because Tom wanted to be at a match in good time,' said PJ.

Manager Kevin McCooey added that it would either be himself or his brother Aidan, 'another football fanatic', that would collect Tom and drive him to many of the games.

'I remember Kevin's brother Aidan arriving at the house, and collecting him at one o'clock to go to the various matches. He wouldn't miss a Sunday game if Monaghan were playing, unless he was away on tour in England,' added PJ Granaghan.

Tom also talked to me in 2004, during a lazy, warm but hazy Saturday afternoon in his Oram home, about other sports and pastimes, but none seemed to garner the same passion or the same degree of loyalty as Gaelic football did from Tom.

'I played a bit of golf from time to time, and Rose loves to play golf, but for me, I discovered that if you take a break from the golf for a while – as I did often when we were playing with the band – then you lose your golf buddies. Indeed, it probably was the bit of craic and banter that I had with the people that I played golf with that mattered most of all to me. But when you lose that, it takes a while to get into it again – and I never really got back into it. Sure the few bob you might win was only a bonus,' he laughed.

Tom wasn't too interested in the 'few bob' when the local GAA club needed a few acres to extend their football pitch and facilities near Tom's home. It was the late 1970s, and funds were hard to come by, and he had the ideal piece of land near the pitch that the club required.

According to a story in the sports pages of the *Sunday Independent* of 22 April 2018, written by Tommy Conlon, the Oram footballers were sure that Tom McBride would be there to support them every step of the way.

'And when we went to him,' recalls Oram PRO Tony Graham, 'Tom said, "Take whatever yiz want boys, we'll not worry about the money." That typified the generosity of both Tom and Rose towards their local community.'

Tommy Conlon continued: 'Fifty years in showbusiness didn't diminish one whit his love for Gaelic football. He followed the fortunes of Oram and Monaghan until the end. Oram is a tiny rural enclave outside the town of Castleblayney. In 1963 Tom captained them to a Monaghan county junior league and championship double.

'It was a once-in-a-generation achievement for the club. He was a high-fielding, big-boned and square-shouldered mid-fielder. By 1966, his Sunday afternoons in the jersey were replaced by Saturday nights in a showband suit.'

In the concluding remarks in his column, 'The Couch', Tommy added a humorous quote 'to his midfield partners', attributed to Big Tom, about it being a long way from 'Four Country Roads' or 'The Sunset Years Of Life' to playing football.

'I'll go for the high ones, gosson, and you stay down for the low ones,' is what Tom is reputed to have said to some of his former teammates. 'Now if someone had put a tune to that, he'd surely have sung it,' stated Tommy.

While this story about Tom's generosity to his local football club was written in a national Sunday newspaper shortly after Big Tom had passed away, another story had been written years earlier, back in 1972, in another Sunday paper, the *Sunday Press*, as well as in local papers in his home area.

The story from 1972 went under the headline 'Big Tom Rescues Oram'. It began by saying that it was 'great to see' that a man like Big Tom McBride, who 'had done well for himself' in other fields, had come to the rescue of his old club, Oram, providing them with a much-needed playing field.

'For several years now, the Oram club has had to use the Castleblayney pitch for their home matches, but that is now at an end.

'What a pity that other ex-players of other clubs would not follow the fine example of Big Tom and come to the aid of their old clubs who provided them with games and opportunities for playing and entertainment when cash was not so plentiful with them,' stated the *Sunday Press* story.

It added that 'several other players, especially from poorer rural clubs' were now doing well in America and in England, but had never shown the slightest interest in the clubs that nurtured them and provided them with their Sunday entertainment for so many years.

'The attitude of these former players seems to be that they were doing the club an obligement rather than vice-versa. We say "well done Big Tom" and many thanks for your fine example,' concluded the report.

Local newspapers in Monaghan and Cavan, as well as in Kerry, all highlighted a game between Kerry and Monaghan on a Friday evening on Oram's pitch in the 1980s. This was a fund-raising game, as the club was trying to raise money for floodlights for the pitch. True to form, the Oram GAA Club President – who was 'none other than Big Tom' – was playing with his band The Travellers, at a fund-raising dance for the club that night in The Glencarn Hotel, Castleblayney. Both the Kerry and Monaghan teams were to be in attendance, according to the newspaper stories.

'There are more roads leading to Oram and the Glencarn Hotel in Castleblayney this Friday night than to Glenamaddy,' stated one local newspaper story, of course referring to Tom's then-famous song about the four country roads.

Kerry were the All-Ireland football champions then. The team line-up shows that they had some of their best-known players ever on that team, but Monaghan had a few players who had made national headlines too.

One newspaper report on the game stated that 'Big Tom was a capable footballer himself'. He had partnered Tony Loughman (father of the then-star with Monaghan Declan Loughman) at mid-field on the Monaghan junior side of the 1960s. This article also stated that Tony, 'now a showband impresario', was once the manager of the Monaghan team.

'The Oram club have the services of Tom's nineteen-year-old son Dermot, a fine footballer whose six-foot frame is one of the reasons why his club has had an unbeaten run of seven games.

'The go-ahead club is erecting floodlighting for training, and the proceeds from the match and the dance will go towards that end,' stated a local newspaper report.

For those fans of Big Tom who also have an interest in Gaelic football, and there are many of them, this is the Kerry All-Ireland-winning team that was picked to play in Oram, full of household names at that time: 1. Charlie Nelligan; 2. John O'Dwyer; 3. Tom Spillane; 4. Micky Spillane; 5. Tommy Doyle (Captain); 6. John Keane; 7. Sean Stack; 8. Jack O'Shea; 9. Ambrose O'Donovan; 10. John Kennedy; 11. Ogie Moran; 12. Pat Spillane; 13. Micky Sheehy; 14. Timmy O'Dowd; and 15. Ger Power.

They were faced by a Monaghan fifteen that also featured many star players, including Nudie Hughes and Declan Loughman. The Monaghan fifteen was: 1. Paddy Linden; 2. Declan Loughman; 3. Gerry McCarville; 4. Sean McKenna; 5. Bernie Murray; 6. Kieran Murray; 7. Gerry Hoey; 8. Davy Byrne; 9. Hugo Clerkin; 10. Ray McCarron; 11. Eugene O'Hanlon; 12. Nudie Hughes; 13. Mick O'Dowd; 14. Eamon Murphy; and 15. Eamon McEneaney.

In a different story illustrating Big Tom's love of football, by the well-known journalist and broadcaster Patsy McArdle in the *Top Rank News* magazine of March 1973, his success on the playing fields is also documented.

'In the early years, Tom's love of the outdoor life and his rugged affection for country living endeared him to his own community and involved him with his parish football club, which was Oram. A sturdy footballer, he played with distinction with his club team and was also a popular selection for the Monaghan County fifteen on a number of outings.'

'Football is still my favourite sport, although I don't have much time for it now – even to go to a game or watch it on television,' said Tom in the interview with Patsy.

The story added that 'Midweek is the only time he is able to catch a few hours off' to have a game of golf – or go out for a country stroll. 'I love the country air – it does you the world of good,' said Tom.

I interviewed Big Tom's long-time manager and friend Kevin McCooey for this book, on the day of Big Tom's month's mind anniversary Mass. On that same Sunday, Monaghan Senior footballers beat the fancied Tyrone in the Ulster Championship opening game of 2018. With the Monaghan Minors winning too, Kevin felt that there may have been some divine intervention involved.

'I think that maybe Tom and Rose were up above, looking down on us, and they too rowed in with Monaghan for that two-points win over Tyrone,' he said.

Football remains an integral part of life for all the McBride children and grandchildren. One passionate footballer among the younger grandchildren is Glen Forde, who, at only eleven, is regarded as a great prospect in the Oram under-age teams. His mother Siobhán jokingly says that she believes he only goes to school to play football, and that he is similar to his famous grandfather in that respect!

Another grandson of Tom and Rose, Jason Duffy, who is still only twenty, has already had a number of outings with the Armagh Senior team. He also plays with the football team in Jordanstown University, where he is a student. His mother, Aisling, says that brothers Gavan is also a promising young footballer with middle brother Conor adopting the rugby code with Dundalk RFU as well as being a keen fisherman.

Big Tom's eldest son, Thomas, also showed great promise as a minor county player with Monaghan, and his son Stephen is another talented footballer in the family. Dermot McBride also excelled as a player in younger years, and his son Kieran shows signs of following in his footsteps too as well as being a keen boxer also. While Dermot still loves football, he always had an interest in horses while growing up, and he still retains that interest in horse racing.

However, even though he owned a racehorse at one time, Big Tom said, in the interview with *Top Rank News* in March 1973, that he wasn't a gambler, and would rarely bet on racing.

'I only place a few bets in the whole year – at the Grand National or some other big race,' said the big man.

Back in his home in Oram, during the August afternoon spent interviewing him in 2004, Big Tom told me about how golf, along with some other pastimes, became favoured by him when his football playing days were long gone past. Tom played golf to relax, particularly on a Monday, after a busy schedule over the weekend – his golfing reached a high standard with a single figure handicap.

Tom also loved to play snooker, and had his own full-size snooker table installed in a purpose-built building beside his home. He would spend many long hours, mostly in the winter time, playing snooker with his

Horsing about: Tom with his horse, Fergie, and jockey Johnny (Gerry) Carvill. A young Dermot McBride is pictured front left, and Tom's wife Rose is on the right.

friends to the wee small hours. The interest in snooker spread to the family and also further afield, with seven-times world champion Stephen Hendry once visiting Tom's home while on a visit to Castleblayney.

The beautiful Lough Muckno in Castleblayney also provided Tom with another sporting outlet in the form of water skiing. In fact he was one of the first people to water ski on the lough.

From one water sport to another, fishing was also a great pastime for Tom who even tied his own flies.

'I like to do a bit of fishing too, and in the last lot of years I've done a right bit of fishing, especially around the west of Ireland – in the River Moy in Mayo in particular, and way out west towards Belmullet and the Bangor Erris area. It's great for relaxation,' he told me.

He also said that he and a great friend and fan, PJ Granaghan from near Ballina, would often meet when Tom and a group of fishermen from Monaghan would go to North Mayo to fish. PJ says he has many memories of those visits.

'He fished around Belmullet, Bangor Erris, Ballina and Pontoon, and there would always be a group of them together from Monaghan, who were all keen fishermen. He also loved to fish in the famous Ridge Pool in Ballina, where former Irish soccer chief Jack Charlton used to fish.

'Tom and the TV star Derek Davis were also two fishermen, and they enjoyed going out on the lakes and rivers together to fish,' added PJ.

Tom the fisherman: Relaxing with rod and line on the river.

Indeed Tom's pastime of fishing was featured on an RTÉ television programme presented by his pal, the late Derek Davis. Derek was by then one of the best-known faces on Irish television, but he actually started out his career doing a parody of Big Tom.

Derek started out in showbusiness under the stage name of Mean Tom, and he sang for a while with the showband The Tree Tops, from Cork. The entertainment magazine *New Spotlight* heralded the arrival of Mean Tom, in a story about how 'a mixture of two Cork bands' had hired 'a lumbering giant from the North who looks the spit of Big Tom'.

The story went on to say that while it was an unusual combination, 'it's potent and went down well'.

'Mean Tom was brought in as a gimmick, but he stopped the band in its tracks when they, and he, both discovered that he could in fact sing.

'Nobody had expected him to be able to sing – the fact that he looked like Big Tom's younger brother was enough for most people. But out of this strong man came sweetness ... and big Mean Tom turned out to be a honey-voiced version of Big Mean Johnny Cash,' stated the story.

While the article went on to say that Mean Tom and the band were doing well in rural areas, they had at that early stage avoided the big cities. 'We haven't played in Dublin with Mean Tom yet' noted manager Mark Nodwell. 'The city promoters don't seem to take us seriously, so we'll just sit back and wait till they do.'

But it seems that many promoters didn't take Mean Tom seriously as a singer. After a short sojourn with the Cork band, Derek Davis went back to journalism, and eventually to RTÉ. He was well known as a newsreader, and later as a popular presenter of television programmes, including co-hosting the top-rated 'Live at Three' show with Thelma Mansfield.

So when he was trying to mimic Big Tom as 'Mean Tom' with The Tree Tops, the late Derek never made it in the world of country music. However, shortly before retiring from television, he even went to Nashville and recorded an album, entitled *My Heart's On the Road*. By a strange quirk of fate, that recording was organised by his then-agent, the late Tony Loughman from Castleblayney. Tony's Top Rank agency had Big Tom and The Travellers on their books for many years, and of course Derek and Big Tom became firm friends as well as great fishing buddies.

Tom's friend Carl Laverty says that the singer was an all-round sportsman. One memory that he has of him is at the opening of the local Concra Wood Golf Club.

'There Tom was, singing on the shores of Lough Muckno with the two late great golfers Christy O'Connor Junior and Senior. They described it afterwards as the best night's entertainment they had ever enjoyed,' says Carl.

Paddy King says that his sister Rose and his brother-in-law Big Tom McBride were big-hearted people, who loved sport as well as music.

'They were great people, and above all else they cared about others, including all who played football with the Oram club in particular. We had many great nights at the local community centre, as well as on the road with The Travellers. There was always plenty of good craic too with Tom and Rose and the family when they had the Log Cabin pub. I remember them too for their golfing, as they were both good golfers – at one stage, Tom played off nine. Rose was a good golfer too, and she loved that new course here near the town – she enjoyed going there so much,' says Paddy.

Paddy also says that the link with sport that Big Tom and Rose had with Oram lived on to the end of their days. This was beautifully highlighted in the way the local GAA club played such a big part in Tom's funeral, with his body being laid out in the community centre, where thousands of neighbours and admirers filed past his coffin.

'Their memories will live on. Young people came up to me after the funeral and said they never knew that Tom was such a massive celebrity that even the President of Ireland came down here to pay his respects. These were young men and girls who said to me they didn't know how big a star they had living in their midst, and that was because Tom was so humble about it all,' said Paddy.

He also said that President Michael D. Higgins's visit, to convey the sympathy of the nation to the family, is something that they, the whole community and the people who followed Big Tom, will never forget. As well as the serious and solemn moments when the President came to pay his respects, they had plenty of light-hearted moments too at the GAA clubhouse that Big Tom had helped fund-raise for over the years.

'I was asked to introduce President Higgins to some of the players from the Oram GAA team who were doing the Guard of Honour, and we shared a few laughs during that too.

'When I was walking him down through the team, I would say something like, "This is Sean, and he's not a bad footballer; he can catch a pint now and again too, especially on a Saturday night!" While I might say that this next fellow in the line is a great footballer, or jokingly that this next lad is not too good; and then I would go on and say that "I don't know this fellow's name at all"! The President knew that I was winding up some of the lads, including one of my own sons, and he had a good laugh at that.'

Paddy added that it was such a great honour to the memory of Big Tom for the family and the whole community that the President came down to pay his respects personally, both in the GAA centre and at the McBrides' home.

'He could easily have just sent a telegram, or phoned, but he came down here in person, and in the family's time of grief that was so comforting. It is something that we will never forget. He is a sincere man, and I will vote for him again. I'm sure so will all the people around here, the GAA fans and so also will all Big Tom fans,' said Paddy.

Big Tom was laid out for one of his final days on this Earth in the Oram clubhouse that he loved so well, during the unseasonably warm days at the end of April 2018. It was also at this GAA pitch and centre that a plaque was unveiled in his honour over a decade earlier – also in bright sunshine.

But when Big Tom got up to speak on that evening, it was obvious that he was flabbergasted when he saw a plaque unveiled in his honour at the GAA centre. Even in the bright sunshine, he wasn't singing 'You Are My Sunshine' for those behind the erection of the plaque.

'I only found out about this late last year, and to those people who were responsible for it – well, when I heard about it, I swore I'd kill them,' said Tom with a smile.

As the sun shone down, this shy superstar spoke to the huge crowd that had travelled from all over Ireland for the unveiling of his image on the wall outside Oram GAA pitch.

'I just don't know why such a thing would be erected about me,' he added, but his words were drowned out as the crowd shouted in unison, 'Because you're the greatest!'

One couple came all the way from New Ross in County Wexford for the unveiling. 'That's how much we love Big Tom,' said the woman from Wexford. Meanwhile two other men, who were life-long fans, said they felt honoured to be there, and one of the men reminisced about when he first saw Tom and The Mainliners play.

'I can still see him coming out on stage in a black suit, and The Mainliners were known as the band with the magic beat for dancing.' His friend said that going to Big Tom's home in Oram was similar to going to Graceland. 'I had my photo taken at Elvis Presley's gate in Graceland, and I've lived my dream today as I've got my photo taken with the King outside his gates in Oram,' said the ecstatic fan, in an interview shown on RTÉ's 'A Little Bit Country'.

One month after he passed away, family, friends, neighbours, fans and GAA members gathered again at Oram GAA Community Centre to share many fond memories, and for a cuppa, following Big Tom's month's mind anniversary Mass. It was on a Sunday afternoon in May 2018. Tom's beloved Monaghan had beaten arch-rivals Tyrone in an Ulster championship game that very same afternoon. Some of those inside the centre watched the replay of Monaghan's winning scores over and over again, on a television screen located behind the bar. As they sipped their drinks, a few remarked that Tom and Rose were looking down on both the Monaghan Senior and Minor teams that day.

At the end of the hall, a mural of Tom playing his guitar stands tall on the gable wall, with a list of his hit albums and singles painted on either side.

Outside, as the Sunday summer sun was setting, some of his grandchildren were still practising their football skills, knocking goals and points into the goalmouth on the community centre side of their pitch, where Big Tom once played. A month earlier, at his funeral, those grandchildren proudly carried an Oram GAA flag, their granddad's gold disc, his guitar, and his fishing rod and family photographs to the altar of the little church across the road.

The previous year, when 'Nationwide' presenter Mary Kennedy remarked about the Monaghan flag flying proudly in the front garden of Tom's home, just a short distance up the road, she asked if he 'had high hopes' for Monaghan football.

'Of course we always have high hopes for Monaghan football, but they never seem to materialise – however, we live in hope,' said Tom. Perhaps his grandchildren, carrying on that proud family football tradition, will see those hopes of the singing star, who was firstly a football star, realised someday in the future.

Just as fans of the famous poet and prose writer Patrick Kavanagh have been calling for years to nearby Inishkeen to see the place he left for Dublin in 1939, fans of Big Tom come to Oram, to see his home, the fields where he farmed and the halls that he played in, as well as his local football field of dreams.

Kavanagh, for a time, farmed Monaghan fields too. He wrote about 'boys in their bicycles going to dances', but Patrick Kavanagh and Big Tom never met. The literary genius died in 1967, just as the singing star was climbing the charts. The bicycles taking boys and girls to dances were fast being replaced by motor cars and motorcycles.

Retired RTÉ television 'Sunday Game' presenter Jim Carney referred to both Patrick Kavanagh and Tom McBride in an article in the *Tuam Herald* recently. He stated that 'one of Ireland's greatest poets [Kavanagh] was also his local football team's goalkeeper'.

'Music and sport are hugely popular in Monaghan. The renowned country singer Big Tom McBride was a powerfully built defender too with his local football team Oram. One of his team managers once compared him to the legendary Cavan footballer Big Tom O'Reilly and so, naturally, the Oram player also became known as Big Tom,' stated Jim.

So Patrick Kavanagh and Big Tom McBride had much in common – both were sportsmen; both started out tilling the stony grey soil of the fields of Farney (the mediaeval Gaelic name for Monaghan). They were both country boys from the drumlin county who travelled on bicycles the hilly, winding rural roads to dances in their teenage years.

Later they progressed to the pinnacles of their professions – bards they were both.

Chapter 5

Lonely Emigrants in London

Lonely nights in London are hard to comprehend

But easy to a stranger in a foreign land

The money's good with things you could never do at home

But empty chairs and winding stairs ring a hollow tone

'Lonely Nights in London', Margo O'Donnell (written by MJ Clarke)

This song about emigration to the UK in the 1950s and 1960s, albeit it from County Clare, could just as easily refer to an emigrant from Castleblayney such as Big Tom. The country 'n' Irish song – sung by several, but especially popular for Margo O'Donnell – is not to be confused with an album of the same title by Eric Bell of iconic rock group Thin Lizzy!

Escape from the Snipegrass, a film made in Mayo in the late 1950s and screened later by RTÉ, was prophetic of a path that awaited many emigrants such as Big Tom in that era. The 'GNR Steam Train' (which he would later sing about) took him to what may have been a lonely life in London. Perhaps the words of one of his lesser-known songs, which he co-wrote, sum up this loneliness.

I left like many more
Came over to England in late '64
My father and mother begged me not to go
How I wish I had listened to them years ago.

'My Own Lisnagreive' (H. McMahon/T. McBride)

Emigrating in the late 1950s and working laying cables in Scotland, also in a Walls ice cream factory in London, plus a stint picking tomatoes in Jersey, Tom McBride may have experienced the loneliness of an emigrant, but he experienced friendship too. And this resulted in him getting 'all' the words of his first hit, 'Gentle Mother', via two of his flatmates, from their sister in Ireland.

In an interview in the front room of his home, on a balmy August Saturday evening in 2004, Tom told me about how he had got his lucky break with this song while in London all those years earlier.

'Apart from those three years or so that I was away in England and Scotland, finishing up in Jersey in the Channel Islands, I've lived here in Monaghan all my life. I had a brother at home who died young, and as he was the only son at home then, that is why I came back home to Castleblayney, to help work the farm.

'I had learned some songs and music while in London, and had got to know how to play a bit on the guitar. Some of us would get together in the flats over there, and we would sing a few songs and swap some songs as well,' said Tom.

'That is where I got my first song, "Gentle Mother". It came from some Monaghan fellas that I was staying with over in London. One night in the flats, they sang a verse and a chorus of "Gentle Mother", and when I heard it, I asked if they knew the rest of the song. They said they had a sister at home who knew all the song, and so I put one of the lads to the trouble of writing to the sister in Ireland to get the rest of the song words. That was a lucky break for me.'

In an interview with Pam Jackson, for Hugh O'Brien's 'Hot Country' Sky television show in 2011, Tom says the break in London happened by 'pure chance'. He also said that when he came home to Ireland, he suggested the name The Mainliners for the band that he was to front. But this idea came from a band he used to listen to while an emigrant in Jersey.

'I often went to listen to a band named The Mainliners while I was working in Jersey, and that's where the name came from for our band later. So I swiped the name,' he added.

But firstly, after coming home, he joined a band called The Blue Seven, before moving to a group called The Finncairn that were originally playing a lot of Céilí music. The Finncairn went through two name changes – firstly to The Mighty Mainliners, and then shortening the name to become simply The Mainliners. They all lived in the one area, which was handy for getting together to practise, as they could almost cycle to rehearsals! 'And perhaps sometimes some of us did cycle to a few of our practices,' he told me in our 2004 interview.

'I suppose how we got together was because we were all from Castleblayney, or not further than about five miles away. The two McMahons,

Henry and Seamus, lived almost beside us, and that was only three miles from Castleblayney. John Beattie lived in the town, as did Ginger Morgan and Ronnie Duffy. Cyril McKevitt would have been the only import, and he came from about five miles outside Castleblayney. At the beginning for rehearsals it was great, it was so handy.'

The rehearsals were usually in the home of the McMahons, and Tom played 'a bit of saxophone and a bit of guitar', as well as doing some singing. Looking back on that time, Tom says that the parents of Henry and Seamus were very tolerant, allowing them to practise their tunes in the front room of their home!

'We started to rehearse very local, mostly in the sitting room of Henry and Seamus McMahon's home. I don't know how their parents put up with it. The mother and father, God rest them both, never said a thing to us. There was many a night's craic in that house, and plenty of noise.

'Then if we got a gig somewhere, we would probably go early to the venue and get the sound set up and rehearse for an hour or so in the hall that we were going to play in that night,' Tom told me.

They were playing at one of the local dinner dances when they were heard by a man named John McCormick. McCormick was well known in the Monaghan area, promoting dances at the Maple Ballroom in Rockcorry, which was a few miles outside Castleblayney. He was soon to become their manager.

'John offered to get us a few dates. He worked very hard for us to eventually get us a spot on a TV programme called "The Showband Show", and I suppose you could say that we really took off after that,' said Tom.

The man who would become known as the King of Country, or the Gentle Giant of Country, was not the lead singer with the band at first.

Ginger Morgan had written a pop song titled 'Thinking of You', and this was the planned promotional song on the double-A-sided single MD1060, on the Emerald Record label.

'We had been playing together as a band for a while when the idea of recording some songs came to mind. Ginger was into the music, and he decided that he would write the song that he would sing on our first record. It was a very good song too, and was very popular, but the song that took off when the record was released was the B-side, which was "Gentle Mother". That record did a hell of a lot for us since,' said Tom.

Tom said that he never got tired of singing 'Gentle Mother'. He described it as 'a lovely song with a lovely story to it, as everybody has a mother. That song also had a nice air to it.'

In that 'Hot Country' television interview back in 2011, Pam Jackson asked what his thoughts were when he first heard himself singing it. Tom replied that he thought it wasn't his voice at all!

'The first time I heard myself singing it was on a record, but we had no record player in our home at that time. Our manager John McCormick took both the disc, which we had recorded in Dublin, and the record player, to our house, so that we could listen to it.

'John set up the record player in our kitchen, and when he played the song, my first reaction was to say that it wasn't me that was singing. I thought it didn't sound like me at all, but it was, and that song put us on the road.'

But did it change his whole lifestyle? I asked Tom this during our interview in his home, twenty-eight years after he had that first hit. He laughed out loud as he replied.

'Well, it certainly changed what was in our pockets. At the time we were playing small gigs – small halls and dinner dances – and we played many

Celebrating the success of 'Gentle Mother' with parents, neighbours and friends.

nights for five pounds. It was only on an odd occasion that we might get six or seven pounds for the night. However, once the song was on TV's "Showband Show" and got a few plays on radio, people liked it and they started coming in bigger numbers to hear us wherever we played.

'We got to play in bigger venues and I remember the first time we got ten pounds for playing a gig was at a carnival dance not far from our home area, which was a huge success. We felt we were on our way, as we were starting to go well at that stage,' he added.

Tom also said in that interview that he never could analyse why the song became such a hit, or why he became so inextricably identified with it.

'A lot of people have asked me the question down through the years, why did I think I was successful with it? But I could never put a finger on that.

Some would say to me that it was the way we did the song, as there was a lot of sentimentality in it, and it came across in our version. But I don't really know – perhaps it is something like that. It was just something that happened for us, and a lot of people would say to me that I have a voice with a bit of a tear in it. While I honestly don't know why that song worked so well for us, all I can say is that it started something that stayed with us down through the years.'

Regarding songwriting, Tom said that while he co-wrote 'a few', he always found it difficult. He added that it was his view that 'you have to be a bit of a poet to write a song', and he always 'got stuck after the first verse or two'. But he talked about how the songwriting talent of Mainliners band-leader Henry McMahon was to emerge later. He also spoke in that interview fourteen years ago about Henry's skills as a musician, as well as his work ethic and business acumen.

'There is no doubt about it but Henry came up with some great songs for many singers. Songs such as "Your Wedding Day" for Jimmy Buckley, which was a huge song for him in recent times. He wrote "The GNR Steam Train" for me much earlier than that, and "My Own Lisnagrieve", and of course other very big songs, such as "The Nearest to Perfect" for Michael English, while "The Marquee in Drumlish" was a huge song for Declan Nerney.'

Talking during that interview about the energy and enthusiasm that Henry continued to have for the music business down through the years, Tom remarked, 'He is still flying.'

'He is always on the go, and if Henry came to visit you, he might have time to drink a cup of tea or he might not. He could be rushing off to somewhere else that he had to go to, or to something that he had to do. He's always on the move; there is great push in Henry. He was always one

ig Tom McBride, the King of Monaghan Junior Football, 1963.

Top left: Big Tom on his Confirmation day, with his sister Madge (left), Mary Rafter (right) and another neighbour, Samuel McBride (back).
Top right: The youthful Madge and Tom McBride beside a farm gate near their home.
Right: Big Tom working in the fields with neighbour Hugh McMahon.
Below: The Mainliners during the height of their success picture on the shores of Lough Muckno. Left to right: John Beattie, Seamus McMahon, Ginger (Jimmy) Morgan, Big Tom (front), Ronnie Duffy, Cyril McKevitt and Henry McMahon.

Above: A happily windswept family, wagon wheel and all.

Left: Rose and Tom in the garden of their house in Oram.

Below: Big Tom with his first big car.

Some of the many albums and singles recorded by Big Tom, beginning with (left) the song that really got the ball rolling, 'Gentle Mother'.

Above: Between the brass boys. Cyril McKevitt on trombone and Henry McMahon on sax surround Big Tom as he plays rhythm guitar.
Right: On board – Big Tom and Johnny McCauley on the *QE2*, en route to the USA in 1980.
Below right: In Nashville, backstage at The Grand Ole Opry, with another country music legend – singer and songwriter Stonewall Jackson, who had thirty-five chart hits in the USA during his career.

Above: Big Tom, little Thomas and the family puppy.
Below left: The one that didn't get away! Tom with one of his catches.
Below right: A family gathering – Big Tom with (from left) step-brother Bertie, brother Seamus and sister Madge.

Big Tom the sportsman (clockwise from top left): With one of his racehorses; taking careful aim; speedboating on Lough Muckno, with Ginger Morgan skiing behind; and encouraging his gun dog.

Above: With Tom McGurk and the television crew, recording 'Last House' for RTE in 1976.
Left: With Susan McCann on the shores of Lake Muckno, to publicise her single 'Big Tom Is Still The King'.

man who chased the work, and I often said that he was a great man for chasing the pound – but it's the euro now,' Tom added with a laugh.

Tom listened to many American country singers in his younger days, both at home and in the UK. While Johnny Cash wasn't the first one of those, he became a big fan later on.

'He was a singer that when you heard him once, you never forgot his voice. Another thing about him was that if you heard three words of a song from him on the radio, you knew that it was Johnny Cash. He had that distinctive voice and sound, but sadly he passed away in 2003. He was a big loss to country music. But he made a big impression on so many, and I was one of those who enjoyed Johnny's songs. He was a great ambassador for country music all over the world.'

There are many similarities between the careers of Big Tom and Johnny Cash, and between their lives too. Both had brothers who died young – Johnny's brother in a chainsaw accident; Tom's brother from meningitis. Johnny and his wife June were inseparable in life, and sadly they both died within months of each other. June passed away in May 2003, and Johnny in September of that year. Rose McBride and Tom were a similarly close couple throughout their adult lives. Rose died in January 2018, and only eleven weeks later Big Tom passed away also – many would say from a broken heart.

Perhaps it is strange too that both of them recorded the iconic gospel song 'Far Side Banks Of Jordan', written by Terry Smith, which has a message in its lyric about meeting a loved one in Heaven – possibly prophetic for both singers, as their much-loved lives' partners passed away shortly before them?

Tom said that it was one of his daughters, Aisling, who inspired him to record 'Far Side Banks of Jordan'.

'I heard her singing it at a party, and I asked her if she was going to record it. When she said she wasn't going to do so, she wrote out the words for me. I liked it, and we put it down as a track on the album I Am an Island,' said Tom.

The song is full of thought-provoking words, such as 'when I see you [arrive in the after-life] I'll rise up with a shout'. The singer also says that he/she will run 'through the shallow waters [on the other side] reaching for your hand'.

Interestingly, both June Carter-Cash and Rose King-McBride passed away shortly before their husbands, to be 'waiting on the far side banks of Jordan', as Terry Smith's lyrics seem to suggest.

But while Johnny Cash left the farm work behind, moving away from his home area to become a full-time singer, Big Tom came back from exile in London to the farm, thinking that he would be mixing farming with music for his career.

'I probably wouldn't have become a full-time farmer, as the farm that I was born and reared on was a small holding. While I helped out on it before going away, I would do other work as well. But I never thought that music would be my main career – it was just something that happened for us,' he said with a smile.

'However, I also liked the farming. I suppose if somebody had asked me when I was young if I would like to be a carpenter, or even given me a chance to be one, I probably would have gone down that road in life, while also doing the bit of farm work.'

In an article in the *Irish Independent* on Wednesday, 18 April, the day after Tom's death, Clodagh Sheehy said, 'The guitar that Big Tom McBride bought in London for £12, while still in his teens, was probably the best investment of his life.' How right she was.

Clodagh Sheehy also alludes to Big Tom and The Mainliners' success among Irish emigrants. 'Perhaps even more so the band appealed to huge crowds of emigrants in London, Manchester and Birmingham, and Big Tom quickly became known as the King of Irish country music.'

Writing in the *Sunday Independent* on 22 April 2018, two prominent journalists, Liam Collins and Declan Lynch, tried to analyse Big Tom's style of music. They came up with contrasting answers. Declan stated that the country 'n' western category 'could never really contain him', and country 'n' Irish wouldn't do it either.

'Big Tom was stranger than that, which always made him somewhat interesting to connoisseurs of strangeness,' stated Declan. However, Liam put him firmly in the country 'n' Irish category. 'Big Tom, along with Larry Cunningham and Philomena Begley, were the undisputed champions of country 'n' Irish music,' according to Liam's article.

Now, if you so wish – you, the reader of this book – you can decide for yourself which type of music Big Tom played, taking into account the observations of those esteemed writers. Perhaps the fans of Tom McBride might say it was simply Big Tom music?

Liam Collins, in that article, was clearly not a fan of the songs that Johnny McCauley wrote for Tom, and for other Irish singers:

'His [Tom's] biggest hit of the 1980s came with "Four Country Roads", written by Johnny McCauley, who had a dance band in London and wrote a string of slushy songs name-checking Irish counties like Wicklow, Leitrim, Donegal and other emigrant blackspots,' stated Liam. One assumes that he is referring to 'Lovely Leitrim', the number one hit for Larry Cunningham in the 1960s. But that was written decades earlier, and originally as a sean nós song, and was penned by a mounted policeman in New York named

Phil Fitzpatrick, a native of that county, who was shot dead in a bloody gun battle in the US city in 1947.

During the early years of his career as a singer and recording artist, Big Tom recorded many songs written by the late Porter Wagoner. Apart from being a successful country singer-songwriter and television host in the USA, Wagoner is also credited as the man who launched Dolly Parton to stardom.

Tom's earlier records were often Porter Wagoner songs, and one of those was his second hit song, 'Old Log Cabin for Sale', in 1967. This went higher in the Irish pop charts than 'Gentle Mother', reaching number four and staying for fourteen weeks in the Top 20.

The Mainliners recorded in Ireland, but Big Tom's record label, Denver, was located in London, the city of his youthful working exploits as an emigrant. It was operated by another emigrant, and Tom's great friend, the songwriter Johnny McCauley, who never forgot his own roots in Derry and Donegal. While most of Big Tom's original songs in the 1970s and 1980s were Johnny McCauley compositions, the two men brought out one single on the label that was aimed at the British market. This was an American country-rock hit – but, as always, Big Tom sang it very much in his own style. It was the Crosby, Stills, Nash and Young song 'Teach Your Children'.

'It was another song people probably wouldn't associate me with. However, I liked the song, it had a nice bouncy sound to it and I liked the story, even if it was a complicated story for a country song. Johnny McCauley loved the recording of it, and it was released in England as well as in Ireland.

'But at that stage we were an Irish label [Denver], even if with a base in England. I was an Irish singer, and it was very hard to break into the British music market at that time. Although it did get plays on radio stations in the UK, and it done well enough, it was popular with the Irish people in England, but not popular enough to make the charts, and it didn't break any barriers for us over there,' says Tom.

If he were a singer of lesser honesty, he might have said that it bubbled under the UK charts. But that wasn't Tom's way of talking. He spoke about success, or the lack of it, exactly as it was – with no embellishment of the truth, and no sugar-coating of the story. At that time, Irish country or folk singers had not yet cracked the UK pop charts. It was to be many more years before groups such as The Fureys and Foster and Allen benefited from having hits among mainstream music audiences in the UK. Of course, perhaps the biggest success of all from Ireland in those genres is Daniel O'Donnell, who has filled venues as big as the London Palladium and the Royal Albert Hall.

'In the late 1960s, Big Tom and The Mainliners were famously pack-ing out massive London venues such as the Galtymore and the National. Thirty years later, another Irish band was selling out another London venue – the Royal Albert Hall, no less. It was The Saw Doctors in 1998, and their audience was the next generation, the sons and daughters of many people who'd danced to Big Tom in their day,' stated Tommy Conlon in the Sunday Independent, 22 April 2018.

In his column, called 'The Couch', Tommy added that, musically, The Saw Doctors were coming from 'the opposite end of the spectrum to Country 'n' Irish. And yet it was here that provincial Irish life, GAA included, was recorded in song.'

The Saw Doctors ploughed their own furrow in the UK, with their own Shamtown Records label, over the past few decades. Years earlier, Johnny McCauley's Denver record label had also ploughed a lone furrow for Irish country music in London, when Big Tom was contracted to the label.

Tom and his songwriter/record-label-owner friend never signed any contract. But the two men remained firm friends throughout the years, while Johnny was writing hit songs for Tom from his home, named 'Rose Cottage', in London. It is testament to the honesty and integrity of both men that they never fell out over any aspect of the business, and Tom remained Johnny's best friend until he passed away in 2012.

Above and opposite: Two early publicity photographs of The Mighty Mainliners. The contact telephone number is 'Rockcorry 15'!

In a story in the London-based *Irish World* newspaper of 28 April 2018, Chris McCauley is quoted as saying that Tom and his dad had 'a special rapport'. Chris McCauley elaborated on the business partnership. 'I think it says a lot that they never signed a contract, any business stuff was done on trust and the friendship they had between them.

'The last time I met Tom was at my dad's funeral in London. Tom kindly came over and sang "Four Country Roads" at the end of the service. He also sang "My Rose of the Mountain", a song originally written about my grandmother, Rose, but I think he had another Rose in mind when he sang it,' added Chris.

While London may have held some lonely memories for Tom from his time as an emigrant there, the British capital was also the scene of some of his greatest triumphs as a live entertainer. In 1969, following the success of 'Gentle Mother', mounted police had to be deployed to control the crowds filling the streets around the Gresham Ballroom when he played there with The Mainliners. In 2008, when Big Tom and The Mainliners played at the closing dance in the famous Irish ballroom the Galtymore in Cricklewood, huge crowds turned out to see him once again, as current young country superstar Nathan Carter from Liverpool has good reason to recall.

Nathan grew up in a house of Irish country music fans in Liverpool. His grandparents in particular introduced him to the songs of Big Tom, Larry Cunningham, Joe Dolan and Daniel O'Donnell from an early age. Nathan described Big Tom as 'the Johnny Cash of Ireland' on a 'Late Late Show' tribute programme to the King of Country, as well as in numerous other interviews. Nathan also said, in an interview with Siobhán Breatnach in the *Irish Post* newspaper in London, that while he grew up listening to his music in Liverpool, he never met Big Tom until he got the call to play support to him at the closing-down gig in the Galtymore in 2008.

'I'd grown up with his music in our house. My nan and granddad were huge Big Tom and The Mainliners fans. We had a lot of cassette tapes, and I remember looking through them. Songs such as "Four Country Roads", "Gentle Mother" – all the old hits.'

'I hadn't got to meet him until the night I got to support him in 2008, when the Galtymore closed. Of course, my nan and granddad would have danced to him in Liverpool and different places, and in London. I'd never been at a dance with so many people – there were maybe 3,000. For me at the time, it was a huge gig, and to meet Big Tom before he went on stage was a huge honour. I got my picture taken with him, and it was amazing to see all the people at the front of the stage. There must have been three or four hundred people just gathered round the front of the stage in masses, all with huge respect for this man,' said Nathan.

'They knew every word to every song. You could tell that the songs meant a lot. Big Tom was bringing a bit of their home county back to them in London. You could really see this. He just seemed a humble and very kind man, very simple in his ways. He didn't seem to be one for a big, flashy light show or big staging. He just got up there and sang his songs.'

Nathan was only eighteen at the time, and he had the daunting task of going on before Big Tom and The Mainliners. Nathan was also singing his songs with just a keyboard in front of him.

'I didn't get to speak to him for long that night, but I did a couple of gigs with him since,' said the young star, who talks about their other meetings elsewhere in this book. Nathan has been including a medley of Big Tom songs at his concerts around Ireland, as a way of paying tribute to his songs and his career.

As Nathan Carter gathered, and rightly so, the crowds in the Galtymore had been even bigger in previous decades, when Big Tom played there fre-quently. This is illustrated in a story from a dancer, Máire Ní Gioblain, who 'lived and worked for most of her life in London', but is now retired to Galway. She met her husband Tim in London, according to the book *From the Candy Store to the Galtymore* (Ballpoint Press, Bray, 2017).

'We witnessed great nights in the "Galty". I recall the night we tried to get in to see Big

Big Tom 'plays' a guitar-shaped mirror at the Galtymore Ballroom in London.

Tom. The crowds were massive, four deep and while we managed to get as far as the ticket desk where we paid our money that was as far as we progressed. The audience was so jam-packed inside we couldn't get past the foyer. I said we'd try the Banba instead.

'At the ticket desk they refused to return our money until I explained that I would call the police as the "Galty" that night was a safety hazard. We quickly got our refund after that.'

The crowd at the Galty might have been massive back then, and it was big too on its closing night, but the biggest crowd of all for Big Tom assembled in Roundwood Park, Willesden, on a summer Sunday afternoon in 1979. Here he would headline to over 80,000 people.

Tom and the band were the main act for the London-Irish Festival that year, and they also recorded the gig and created a live album from it. The photograph on the back of that album, taken from the stage, shows the massive attendance at the event – one of the biggest ever among the Irish community in London down through the decades.

Danny Maher, CEO of the community centre, Ashford Place in Cricklewood, described Big Tom's passing as a 'very sad day' in a tribute, also in the *Irish Post* newspaper.

'Big Tom played at the iconic Galtymore so many times, himself and The Mainliners, and on the venue's closing night too in Cricklewood. The older people were talking about him in our place in glowing terms, with many having seen him play at least once in London or at home in Ireland.

'It's a big loss to our crowd but also tinged with some great memories of the dance halls and the Irish country music. It kept them going in the good times and the hard times,' added Danny.

Another Danny, Daniel O'Donnell, was seen by many as the next big Irish star among the emigrants in England, decades after the late Larry Cunningham and the late Big Tom were tops on that circuit in the 1960s and 1970s. Daniel has also spoken glowingly about Tom's affinity with his audience, both at home and in the UK. He also highlighted Tom's great connection with his fans in London and elsewhere.

'He reached out to people in Ireland, and those who had emigrated from Ireland, in the days when so many Irish people lived in England, and their whole connection with Ireland was the bands at the weekend in The National, The Forum and The Galtymore, and all the dance halls around London, Manchester and Birmingham', said Daniel in a tribute in the *Irish Post*. Daniel has many other memories of Big Tom, which he shares later in this book. Big Tom also shares his views on Daniel later in this book, in an interview that he did with me for Daniel's international fan club magazine in 2017.

In the mind's eyes of many emigrants, Tom and Daniel – and also Margo, and decades later The Saw Doctors, along with many other Irish singers – painted vivid sound pictures of home. Their songs created a connection when those emigrants were far away. Hence perhaps the reason for the title of one of Big Tom's vinyl albums, recorded in his own studio in Castleblayney in 1992: *Songs of Home and Far Away*.

Through this music, and the heartfelt lyrics, those emigrants were taken back to travelling to, or from, some Irish crossroads, via 'Four Roads'. In the same way, they were taken to or from the N17, or a road similar to it, in the Saw Doctors' hit. The songs were very different in style, but the common denominator was, and still is, that they both transport the emigrant back home, albeit only in memory, to an Ireland that they left behind. Often, from far away, those scenes of home may seem more beautiful and happier than perhaps they were in reality, if one had to eke out a living at home. But in the mind's eye, Tom's songs, even if sometimes sad, could make the emigrant in London or elsewhere feel that they were (even if for a few minutes), back in a happier and more carefree world, in their younger days in the Emerald Isle.

While it might be a slightly more sugar-coated, romanticised vision of home, perhaps it was good therapy for those exiles, transporting them from the mundane world of work in such a busy place as London, Manchester or Birmingham. It could bring them back to a land of innocence and beauty, with its 'Forty Shades of Green', which Johnny Cash wrote and sang about after visiting Ireland in 1959. But then, as the old adage says, 'far away hills are green' – perhaps even a sparkling emerald-green hue if you are an Irish emigrant who is far from home!

In a fulsome tribute to Big Tom in the *Irish Times* newspaper on 18 April 2018, the day after his death, Michael O'Regan stated that Big Tom's songs were 'a lifeline for a dispossessed people, forced out of their own country, which could not even provide them with the basic human right of a job'.

Michael O'Regan added that while many of his songs were 'melancholic', 'our history of forced emigration is laced with melancholy' anyway.

'He came from Castleblayney, County Monaghan, and knew rural Ireland. He had spent time too as an emigrant in London … They played his records at home and sang his songs at Irish emigrant gatherings, the poignancy of his voice in harmony with the bitter-sweet experience of forced emigration. He understood his audience.

'It is very easy today to dismiss all this as crass sentimentality. It would be wrong, because it was no such thing,' stated Michael O'Regan's in-depth analysis of Big Tom's music in the *Irish Times* article.

Many Irish country stars who have also been popular with the Irish in the UK have paid tribute to Big Tom, and respects paid to the big man from Castleblayney have even extended across to the rock genre. The Edge, guitarist with rock superstars U2 – who long ago took London, the rest of the UK and indeed the world by storm – mentioned Tom to show-biz reporter Eddie Rowley. This was in an interview that Eddie conducted in Tulsa, Oklahoma, after the Irish rock icons had played to over 20,000 American fans. It was published in the *Sunday World* on 6 May 2018.

'Ah, Big Tom,' The Edge said, with genuine warmth and sympathy at his passing. 'I was aware of him when growing up. I wouldn't necessarily have known his music very well, but he was a legend,' added The Edge. By coincidence, on the same Sunday as that interview was published in the *Sunday World*, two weeks after Big Tom's death, the official Irish pop charts in the same newspaper had one of Big Tom's albums – *Greatest Hits, Volume 1* – re-enter the Top 20, just below young superstars of today Niall Horan and Ed Sheeran. Tom's album was ahead of the latest *Gold* collection by the re-formed Abba, ahead of Taylor Swift and ahead of another iconic Irish singer, Christy Moore. Proof, if proof was needed, that even after he had passed on, Big Tom was still up there among the chart hit makers of today.

Chapter 6

Tragedy and Love

Big Tom's big hit 'Back To Castleblayney' was written by his long-time friend, and writer of most of his hits, Johnny McCauley. But Tom McBride's sudden return from the UK to his home town was not a happy one. The untimely death of his brother Willie John, due to meningitis, resulted in Tom coming home from Jersey in the Channel Islands to help his parents manage the family farm.

Willie John was the youngest of the McBride family, and he was the young man who was supposed to take over the running of the family farm.

Tom went into detail about what happened to his brother in an interview with Julie Boyd in *New Spotlight* magazine in the mid-1970s:

'At that time, my seventeen-year-old brother was working on the farm at home, and he had an accident one day, falling off a bicycle. After a year, meningitis set in, and he died. I came home then of course, and never went back.'

Tom also told me that while he eased back into the farming, he 'wouldn't be a full-time farmer', and did other jobs as well.

'After returning home, I teamed up with a friend and we began erecting haysheds, for about £20 a time. That was fairly big money in 1961,' he told Gus Smith in an interview for the *Sunday Independent* eight years later.

Willie John McBride, Tom's younger brother who died of meningitis aged eighteen.

'I started to strum the old guitar again, at home, at parties, weddings and the like. Actually, a couple of local lads asked me to sit in with them in a group.

'We weren't quite sure what we were though, céilí or otherwise. I suppose you could call us half a céilí band,' Tom told Julie Boyd in that *New Spotlight* interview.

He added that the group consisted of himself, George Mackey, Andy Graham and the McMahon Brothers, Henry and Seamus. They called themselves The Finncairn Band.

'Then we kind of broke up, when Henry and Andy decided to go to England. But when the lads returned, we came together again and brought in others,' said Tom.

The others were Ginger Morgan and Ronnie Duffy. Later on, Cyril McKevitt joined them, and after that, the organ player John Beattie. Beattie's distinctive organ sound was one of a number of hallmarks of what was to become known as The Mainliners' magic beat.

Tom suggested they call themselves The Mainliners, the name that he told me he had 'swiped' from a group he heard in Jersey. For a time, they were known as the Mighty Mainliners. But after John McCormick took over as their manager, and after success on 'The Showband Show', a slot that John secured for them, he named them Big Tom and The Mainliners.

The first record, and first hit, for Big Tom and The Mainliners began as something of a slow burner regarding chart success in Ireland. Two stories in Ireland's evening papers at the time, the *Evening Press* and the *Evening Herald*, stated this.

'Already well received and much requested by Irish exiles in different parts of the world, "Gentle Mother" has now been discovered by the record buying public at home,' stated one report, while the other stated that at the end of 1966, the song 'released last July' was now number eight in Ireland's Top Thirty.

According to *The Larry Gogan Book of Irish Chart Hits* (Maxwell Publications, 1987), Big Tom and The Mainliners reached number seven in the Irish Top Thirty with their debut disc, and it stayed for two months in the charts.

Big Tom with The Mainliners' manager for many years, John McCormick (right), and friend John Brown.

The Mainliners' manager, the late John McCormick, produced a promotional leaflet early in 1967, stating the band's pleasure at being up there in the Top Ten with their first record. They were doing battle with such heavy hitters as international stars Tom Jones, The Rolling Stones, The Beach Boys, Cat Stevens and The Monkees. Big Tom was also competing in the higher echelons of the charts with such established Irish stars as Larry Cunningham, Dickie Rock, Joe Dolan and Danny Doyle.

'In January [1967] came Big Tom's first big break; "Gentle Mother" was voted the "Most Requested Record of the Week" on Radio Éireann's (now RTÉ) "Saturday Spin" programme.

'Farmer Tom, well over 6 foot tall, and a County Monaghan footballer, is modest about his success. "I was delighted to get the chance to record in the first place. But to think that 'Gentle Mother' has done so well is very encouraging. Great credit is due to the boys in The Mainliners who supplied the backing for the number," said Tom as he enjoyed his first hit.'

'It was the people around home here that got us going in the first place. They came to see us in the small dance halls, and that's what brought us along,' said Tom in the 2004 interview in his home.

Perhaps if one was to analyse the success of 'Gentle Mother' today, with the benefit of hindsight, it could be said that apart from Tom's voice, 'with a tear in it', the guitar solo at the start by Seamus McMahon, and the organ sounds in the middle by John Beattie, may all have had an impact on its success.

And so this singer, once dubbed 'the hayshed builder turned heartthrob' by journalist Bill Stuart in a national newspaper article, became a hit with the fans with his first record.

But shortly after coming back to Castleblayney, Big Tom McBride must have become a heartthrob too with the young lady who was to be the love of his life – another King, Rose King.

Tom said he first fancied Rose when he saw her and another girl that he knew at a local concert. He contacted the other girl afterwards to see if he and Rose could meet up. With a laugh, Tom said that Rose might have fancied him too, as she agreed that they should meet.

Tom McBride and Rose King in their early courtship days.

After a short courtship, they were married in a wedding with only their bridesmaid and best man at the altar and their parents present.

Rose's brother, Paddy King, remembers them coming back to the house that evening, but the wedding reception there was small and very informal. Paddy, who was only eleven when his sister Rose married Tom, remembers that neighbours and friends came to the house when the newlyweds arrived home. He says the adults had 'a few bottles of stout', and the kids probably got soft drinks and biscuits. But there was 'no big reception as such'. At the time, Paddy probably never even dreamed that someday he would be playing bass and singing in one of Big Tom's bands.

Tom moved to live at the King family home in Oram, and settled down to doing farm work as well as erecting haysheds. But that was before music took over as his main career. Apart from enjoying playing music, Tom always hankered to own a pub. But that was only to come later in his career.

In an interview with Pat Egan in *New Spotlight* magazine in the early 1970s, Big Tom said that erecting haysheds was tough work.

'I used to build haysheds, you know, and it was very hard work. So I'd like to move on to something easy,' said Tom.

But, when his time building haysheds came to an end, Big Tom and The Mainliners slowly but surely worked their way up to a situation where they were often playing six nights a week, all over Ireland and in parts of England. It must have been hard work, and it must have had an impact on his young wife Rose, who was at home minding their children and other older relatives. Their marriage always remained strong though – for fifty-two years.

'Well, I didn't go to the dances in them years, as you couldn't go and leave four children. I had my own parents to mind also, and I was also back and forth to see that Tom's mother and father were okay in their home,' said Rose.

'It was all a full-time job around home in them years,' she told Mary Kennedy in the 'Nationwide' programme on RTÉ television in the autumn of 2017. But she added that she didn't feel any different to all of the other housewives and mothers in her area whose husbands went out to work by day. Tom did the same, except that his work was at night time.

'I never thought of Tom as being a superstar or anything like that, and neither did the children. He was just Tom, who was going off to do another night's work with the band.

'I remember one day when one of the children said in the car that other children at school said that "we had money". My reply was that if that was so, then I haven't seen it,' said Rose.

Back in the 1970s, in a newspaper interview with Father Brian D'Arcy, Rose admitted that, as Tom was away from home a lot at nights, it could get lonely at times. But she added that with the children around her, and the older people, she had 'plenty of company'.

'As long as Tom is enjoying himself, I wouldn't interfere. He says that some-day he'll get out of the business. But I can't see him being able to do without it.

'After we married, he gave up singing for a time, but wasn't happy until he was back at it,' added Rose.

In an interview in 1975 with the *Sunday World*, Rose was asked how she felt about her husband's large female following. She laughed and answered: 'He always comes back.'

Over the years, Rose carefully stored all the trophies, gold and silver discs and awards that Tom had won. With help from the children, she also kept scrapbooks with many of the press clippings and photographs from her husband's illustrious career.

Among those on display in their home were some crystal trophies for Golf Classics in the UK. Tom played in these over eleven years, to help to raise funds for the less-well-off Irish emigrants.

'The bands had their own work to do, but there was always time to fit in a few gigs and a few other events to help people that weren't as well off. It was easy enough to do so, and nice to be able to make a difference,' said Tom.

Right up to the end of their days, both Tom and Rose promoted what she described as 'a fantastic golf course' outside Castleblayney, on the Dundalk Road. I have a vivid recollection of Tom, and especially Rose, encouraging a few of us to visit that golf course before going home to Galway. A group of six of us had stopped off at the McBrides' home in Oram, where we were fêted, and fed with apple pie, buns, cakes and sandwiches at midday on a Sunday. Rose and Tom were the most hospitable hosts you could ever visit. After stuffing our faces with goodies, washed down by cups of tea and coffee, they took us down to the trophy room, where Rose had carefully displayed his awards, 'after years of them being stored in boxes, drawers and presses', said Tom.

His first guitar, accordion and saxophone were on display in the room, and Tom said he had good memories of playing them all, making some humorous remarks about playing the sax.

'Way back at the beginning, a lot of people might not remember now, but I used to play the baritone sax. I had a couple of baritone saxes, but I just played one at a time,' laughed Tom.

Big Tom and The Mainliners' first album, A Little Bit of Country and Irish, released on Emerald Records.

'But then, when I started to sing more and more in the band, I decided that something handier than lifting a saxophone and starting blowing into it might be easier for me.

'The smaller saxophone was handy enough, but some of them baritone . saxes were so big you would nearly need wheels on them to take them around.

'Anyway, I got tired of having to pick up and then leave down the smaller baritone sax, and then change over and pick up a guitar and start singing, so to make life easier, I left the sax aside,' he added.

'For years after that, I continued to play the guitar and sing. That is not to say but I enjoyed playing the sax. I think there is a great lift in the sound of a baritone sax. I stuck to the sax playing for a long time before finally giving it up – but I still kept the singing going,' said Tom with a smile.

He had every reason to keep the singing going, as hit followed hit once 'Gentle Mother' had got the ball rolling for Tom and the band. A best-selling album, titled A Little Bit of Country and Irish and featuring the hit 'Gentle Mother', sold so well, and over such a long period, that several pressings of the record had to be made. Four more hit singles followed, during 1967, 1968, 1969 and 1970. These were the Porter Wagoner song 'An Old Log Cabin For Sale', 'The Old Rustic Bridge By The Mill', 'Flowers For Mama' and their biggest hit up to that point, 'The Sunset Years Of Life'. This spent fifteen weeks in the Top Twenty, peaking at number three in the summer of 1970.

Emerald Records released four more albums by Big Tom and The Main-liners during the late 1960s: *I'll Settle For Old Ireland*, *From Ireland – Big Tom and The Mainliners*, *The All Time Hits of Big Tom and The Mainliners* and *The Sunset Years of Life*.

John Pepper was one of Big Tom's biggest fans, from his childhood days onwards. He later became a close friend of Tom and Rose. John's story about being a follower of Big Tom is a microcosm of so many other fans from all over Ireland – except that his began before he was even old enough to go dancing!

'In 1965–66, Larry Cunningham and Sean Dunphy were the two favourite singers listened to on Radio Éireann in our house. Larry's "Lovely Leitrim", "Tribute to Jim Reeves" and "Among the Wicklow Hills", along with Sean Dunphy's Eurovision entry "When The Fields Are White With Daisies", were firm favourites. That was not only on the Irish Top Ten then, but also on the daily, and nightly, sponsored programmes at the time.

'Then, out of the blue and from nowhere, in 1966, "Gentle Mother" entered the Irish Top Ten and moved up the hit parade. This nostalgic song with sixteen lines was to change our lives forever, and the name Big Tom was soon to assume universal popularity in the world of country music in Ireland and England,' says John.

But as he was only a child at that time, and living near Inniskeen in County Monaghan, John had no chance of getting to see Big Tom and The Mainliners at a dance.

'Inniskeen, County Monaghan, the birthplace of the great poet Patrick Kavanagh, was the venue for a big carnival in June 1966. Although still a young boy at Inniskeen National School, nonetheless I wanted to see Margo and The Keynotes, and Sean Dunphy and The Hoedowners, perform at the carnival. When making the request to my father and mother for permission to go and see Margo and Sean Dunphy, I threw in Big Tom and The Mainliners for good measure, to use as a bargaining trade-off, if necessary! But, unlike Declan Nerney, I did not "get my wish", and I was grounded at home,' says John with a laugh.

MIGHTY MAINLINERS
CASTLEBLAYNEY
Phone Rockcorry 15

Another early publicity photograph of The Mighty Mainliners.

'I was left to sit in the upstairs window of my bedroom and rely on the flow of the river Fane, which originates from Lough Muckno in Castleblayney, flowing through Inniskeen, to carry the music to my ears.

'But I distinctly remember the Monday night that Big Tom and The Mainliners played at that carnival in Inniskeen. Up to then, I'd never seen so many cars, travelling bumper-to-bumper in an endless convoy past our house to Inniskeen. To this day, I have a vivid recollection of that beautiful balmy night in June 1966, when I heard Big Tom live for the very first time, thanks to nature's "sound system", via the river Fane,' says John.

Listening at his bedroom window, he heard each of Big Tom's songs distinctly, and listened to Henry McMahon calling each dance.

'It is an experience I shall never forget. For me, it compared to being at Neil Diamond and Garth Brooks concerts decades later in Croke Park, and Willie Nelson in the Waterfront in Belfast.

'So, as a young boy, I was seduced by what was later to become the phenomenon, Big Tom. Since then, I've never had any inclination to relinquish the addiction that continued to enthral me in the years that followed.'

John says that in the early 1970s, Monday nights were especially important for him. Back then, Radio Éireann had three separate sponsored programmes between the news headlines at 11.00 and the National Anthem, 'Amhrán Na bhFiann', that marked the end of broadcasting at 11.45.

'Big Tom and The Mainliners was one of the sponsored programmes, and, apart from Gaelic football, it became the highlight of my entertainment for the week. With my mother and father gone to bed, I stood on the chair at the kitchen table and pressed one ear against the Pye radio on the shelf, with the volume turned low so as not to disturb the house! During the following fourteen minutes, I was treated to Big Tom's latest releases; updates on their place in the charts. The schedule of the following week's dancing dates for him and "The Band with the Magic Beat" was also announced on that show.'

Finally, John first got to see Big Tom and The Mainliners at a dance in the Pavilion Ballroom in Blackrock, outside Dundalk in Country Louth, in early 1973.

'I'd never witnessed such a queue to get into a dance, and inside it was almost impossible to move. As singer Brian Coll once said, "Big Tom got people to stop smoking at his dances – you couldn't get your hand into your pocket to take out the packet of cigarettes and the box of matches!"

'The scene was no different sixteen years later, on 30 July 1989, in the Oasis outside Carrickmacross, the night that Big Tom and The Mainliners played their first gig after re-forming,' says John.

But for him, the most unforgettable night of all was that dance in Black-rock, when he met and spoke with Big Tom for the first time.

'I was in awe, and felt awkward asking him for his autograph. I could not believe it when Big Tom spoke to me as if he'd known me already. He gave the autograph, shook my hand and thanked me for coming to the dance.

A youthful Big Tom in an early publicity photo.

'This was to become the first of countless occasions when I would travel the length and breadth of Ireland in all seasons to see and hear Big Tom. I would usually remain on at the end of the dance for a word with Big Tom, and to get the coveted autograph again, as if it was my first,' he added.

John says that *The Image Of Me* was the first tape that he bought after starting work in 1972.

'That tape, along with Big Tom's earlier and subsequent releases, such as *Requests*, *Ashes of Love*, *Smoke Along the Track*, became my companions for my journeys, played on the 8-Track car stereo, which was that era's modern version of today's Bluetooth device,' said John with a laugh.

His story is reflective of thousands of other dancers all over Ireland, and many in the UK, who became lifelong fans of Big Tom.

As the 1970s moved on, the dancing crowds just got bigger and bigger for Big Tom and The Mainliners. This was especially true on the carnival-marquee circuit, according to a report in the Sunday Independent by one of its staff writers, Gus Smith:

'At one venue, near Castleblayney, so many turned up that not alone was the marquee filled – the field in which it stood was full too.'

The same writer observed that the singer 'doesn't give great thought to the future' – even though he was clearly told by Tom what his long-term ambition was.

'I would like, though, to buy a good public house when it's all over for me – or perhaps a farm of about 200 acres. I think I'd call the pub "The Old Log Cabin".' Happily, Tom fulfilled that ambition from his words of 1969, and years later he opened his pub in Castleblayney, with that name over its door.

But his time with the Emerald record label was coming to an end, as the 1960s themselves came to an end. Having met London-based songwriter and singer Johnny McCauley, a native of Derry, after a dance in the British capital, Tom started to record some of McCauley's songs. Eventually he was to team up with Johnny's record label, Denver, on which his first hit single was Johnny's composition, 'Back To Castleblayney', in early 1971.

'I would say it was in the late 1960s that I first met Johnny McCauley, one night when we played in The Galtymore Ballroom in Cricklewood, London. Johnny was at the dance, and when we were leaving he came up to me outside the Galty. He told me that he had written a few songs for a singer named Wexford Kiely. That singer died shortly afterwards. He had recorded a popular song called "The Latchico", plus a few others that Johnny had written.

'Johnny said to me that he had some other songs written, and he would like me to hear them. Two of them were "My Own Washing" and "I'll Settle For Old Ireland", and he gave them to me. I recorded them on Emerald at that time. John McCormick, who was managing us then, asked him to write a song for us about going "Back To Castleblayney".

'All that Johnny had to work on, when writing that song, was any information about Castleblayney that John McCormick had given him. He had never been to Castleblayney, up to then. Yet when you see and hear the song he created, out of the few details that he had been given, it proves that Johnny McCauley was a brilliant songwriter.

'He wrote a huge number of great songs for me, and for others as well,' added Tom.

After they had their first Top Twenty hit single on the Denver label with 'Back to Castleblayney', Big Tom and The Mainliners went on to have three number one hit singles in a row on that label. These were 'Broken Marriage Vows' in 1972, 'I Love You Still' in 1973 and 'Old Love Letters' in 1974. During this time, Tom also created recording history by being the first Irish artist to sell over 50,000 copies of an album. That was the phenomenal success of Ashes of Love, which eventually went on to sell over 100,000 copies – but on its release, it was lambasted by one music critic, named Fachtna O'Kelly, in *New Spotlight* magazine.

Talking about the success of that album during our 2004 interview, Tom laughed when that bad review was mentioned. 'I got a very bad review for the record when it came out. I can't remember the bloke's name now, as I haven't heard of him these years anyway.

'He said the album was rubbish, and it would never do anything for us. But maybe it was all the better that he said things like that about it, as the album was a big success for us,' said Tom during our interview. He was clearly in a very conciliatory mood, all those decades later.

Leafing through cuttings from *New Spotlight* magazine, I discovered that the caustic comments by the writer of that very critical review of the *Ashes of Love* album 'enraged' followers of Big Tom and The Mainliners. It resulted in a page of criticism from fans of Tom in the next issue of the magazine.

'His [Fachtna O'Kelly's] review of the singer's latest album *Ashes of Love* seems to have been deeply resented,' stated *New Spotlight* the following week. It published a page of letters – 'a few of the ones we've received' – from readers about the review, with only one backing the review.

'I think that LP was a success too because we covered a very large area of music in it, from songs with perhaps a sad story to the other, more modern, up-tempo songs with bouncy beats, and good dancing tunes as well. I don't know exactly why it was such a massive success. But perhaps it is probably because of the mixture of all that different material that kept us going and kept us there.

'Along with that, when The Mainliners were playing on stage, we did a lot of music that was called "pop" at that time. But whatever people wanted to call it, there is no doubt that it was great music to dance to – the pop music of the 'sixties and 'seventies. We did a fair share of that in our live programme as well. Ronnie Duffy and Ginger Morgan were the singers of those type of songs,' said Tom.

The title track of the *Ashes of Love* album was written back in 1951, by Johnnie Wright and Jack and Jim Anglin. It was recorded by many others, including country rocker Chris Hillman. He was once a member of Los Angeles folk-rock group The Byrds, seen by some music critics as

forerunners of The Eagles. So wasn't it a bit ambitious for Big Tom and The Mainliners to record this song? I asked.

'We did that song our own way. It was very popular for us at the dances, and I still think that it's a great song. We still do it in our live programme, and I think that most people enjoy it.

'I would never try to do a song in the way that someone else did it. We would never try and copy someone else's style. We always did it our own way, and the arrangement that we did, for any song, had to be one that we were happy with.'

Along with the *Ashes of Love* album, all of Big Tom's other record releases were massive sellers in the early 1970s, and the crowds at the dances were bigger all the time wherever he and The Mainliners played. People of all ages came to see them, according to a report by Colin Wood in Mayo's *Connaught Telegraph* newspaper in late 1971:

'I saw them play at many venues during the past year and their drawing power is really amazing.

'What amazed me was the type of patrons that Tom and The Mainliners attracted. I saw old age pensioners pay ten bob [fifty old pence] just to see Big Tom at a carnival in Sligo.

'I talked to the mother of a six-weeks-old baby who took her child with her to a carnival in Kinvara, County Galway, in order to see the genial giant of the showband world. But the sight that will linger longest in my mind is the memory of two girls on crutches who scrambled to meet Big Tom at a Galway ballroom,' states the report.

Undoubtedly, Big Tom and The Mainliners had a 'magic beat' for dancing, and obviously their programme was replicated very well in the best-selling *Ashes of Love* album.

During our 2004 interview, Tom admitted that some of the songs on that record were very modern country for that era, but he insisted that he only sang songs that he liked.

'They probably were a bit progressive, I suppose, at that time. As far as getting radio plays for songs like that back then, it was an impossibility.

'But they were very popular songs for us in the dance halls, even if they weren't played on radio. They were just songs with strong story lines, and they were nice stories, or at least I always thought so. And you know, a lot of them could be true.

'That's why I would record a song – if I liked the story in the song, and if it had a nice melody and a good beat. The beat was important, as we were a dance band – we never really were a showband. The songs that I recorded were ones that I liked.

'I loved the way the Kristofferson song "Sunday Morning Christian" went. I loved the story in that song,' he said.

That song is about somebody who is 'singing louder than the rest' at church on Sunday morning, but who is back to the same old 'wicked ways' come Monday and during the week. 'But surely God will forgive him next Sunday' says a line in the song.

Another track on the *Ashes of Love* album was the Bing Crosby song 'Far Away Places', which, according to one newspaper review at the time, 'gave the album a nice balance'.

During any of my conversations with Big Tom over the years, it was noticeable that he never resorted to using bad language about anything – even on the very rare occasions when he might have to be critical about something. But he humorously departed from his usual clean-talking persona to slightly colour the conversation, albeit slightly tongue-in-cheek, when referring positively to the popularity of two of his own biggest hits.

'I often sing a few songs here in the Log Cabin pub on Monday nights, and "Four Country Roads" is one song that if I didn't sing it, I'd be in trouble. That and the first song that I ever recorded, "Gentle Mother", were two songs you would always get requests for, and you'd get a bollicking if you didn't sing them,' he laughed.

Speaking about requests, Big Tom and The Mainliners tapped into the list of songs most requested at their live shows, and released an album titled Requests in the early 1970s. The Requests album featured all of the band members, and it was a mix of country and pop, plus a few Irish ballads, including the humorous track 'The Little Shirt My Mother Made For Me', featuring band leader Henry McMahon on vocals.

Another very successful album released by Big Tom and The Mainliners during that 1970s wave of popularity was The Image of Me. The front cover featured a photo of Tom sitting on a pillar outside his home, beside the wrought-iron gates with two guitars plus the name Big Tom emblazoned on them. Those gates were a gift to Tom from a dedicated fan. The album Smoke Along The Track was another massive seller for Tom and the band.

I spoke to Robert Mizzell, a modern-day American country singer, who is a big star in Ireland now. Mizzell, a singer born in the USA, the home of country, told me what he feels about the importance of Big Tom in the development of Irish country music.

Robert said that over twenty-five years ago, when he recorded a medley of Tom's three number one hits from the 1970s, as a single and on an album, he hardly knew anything about the King of Irish Country.

'I didn't know Tom at that time, as I was fresh here in this country from Louisiana. But if I had known then what I know now about Tom, I would have got my management back then to push that single a lot more.

'Over the years since then, I've got to know Tom, and the only thing that you could say about Tom was that he was Irish country music. He started it, and as far as I'm concerned, there was no big Irish country star before Tom came along.

'The others all came after him. I realise there were many showband stars here before him, but while lots of other country stars sprouted up after Tom, he was the king,' says Robert emphatically.

Growing up in the little village outside Castleblayney, Big Tom could never have envisaged that his singing would one day lead to over 10,000 people, including the President of Ireland Michael D Higgins, thronging the streets of Oram for his wake and funeral. His friend and neighbour Jim O'Neill says that this just shows the respect that the man had garnered from people all over Ireland and beyond.

'They were all life-long friends and fans, and they always will be,' he says. Jim also says that the people of Oram have steadfastly insisted over the decades that the red rusty tin shed in the village, where Big Tom and The Mainliners started out, should remain standing. It is still there today, on the opposite side of the road to the sloping churchyard where Tom and Rose have now been laid to rest side-by-side, on the gentle slope of one of the little hills of Monaghan.

Chapter 7

Rose Stands By Her Man

She was born King and she married the King, becoming the bride of McBride. While Rose King vaguely knew Tom from schooldays he was a few classes ahead of her and she sometimes said that he didn't go to school too often anyway!

Speaking to Shay Healy on the RTÉ television programme 'A Little Bit Country' in 2006, Tom talked about how he first fancied Rose at a concert in the local hall. Following that, he got another girl, a friend of Rose, to convey the message to her.

'I got in touch with the other girl a few days later, and I asked if she would fix me up with Rose. So those were the first steps that I took to meet Rose. It worked out well – but she must have had her eye on me as well as me having my eye on her,' he laughed.

Tom went on to describe the etiquette of courting in those dancehall days: 'Going to dances was all part of Irish culture at that time, but the era of the ladies lining up one side of the hall, and the men lining up the other side, is long finished now. Back then, you made a race across the floor for the lady that you fancied. But everybody else was in that race too. So if you didn't get the one you wanted, then you wanted the one you got.'

After a short courtship, Rose and Tom walked down the aisle together. They were married by the priest in their local church with only two others, the bridesmaid and best man, at the ceremony. Neighbour Jim O'Neill, who lived beside the King household in Oram, remembers Big Tom coming to 'court' Rose King, sometimes on his bicycle.

'As children, ten or twelve of us from neighbouring families would come to the Kings' house most nights to watch TV. It was the only house in the village that had a TV back then.

'We would know when Tom was there to meet Rose, as his bicycle would be left against the hedge. I remember that a group of us youngsters were at the house on the day that Tom and Rose were married, and we were there when they came back from the church. There was only the four of them at the wedding – bride and groom, bridesmaid and best man, as well as the parents – and they all came back to the house afterwards where we children were watching TV. God rest Mrs King, Rose's mother, as she must have great patience that she didn't chase us all home with a stick,' laughed Jim.

Just as Rose stood by her man that day, she stood by him all through their fifty-two years of married life, through good times and bad. She told Mary Kennedy in a 'Nationwide' television special on Big Tom in the autumn of 2017 that the family never considered themselves any different to their neighbours in the little village of Oram. The only difference was, while most people went to work by day, Tom had to go to work at night, and they all just accepted that.

Rose was there too throughout all of Tom's musical triumphs, from his first hit, 'Gentle Mother', to his three number ones in the early 1970s, when he also became the first Irish singer to sell 50,000 copies of an album. That was his second LP on the Denver label, titled Ashes of Love. One national newspaper at the time calculated that if the LPs were placed one after another, they would stretch all along the road from Castleblayney to Dundalk!

'Rose is gone before her time, and now Tom also, so quickly after her. Thanks, Tom and Rose, for living next door to me. You were both the best neighbours that anyone could ever ask for ... When Rose died, a massive part of Tom went with her; he was lost, dazed and broken-hearted,' said their neighbour Jim O'Neill.

A mere eleven weeks after Father Leo Creelman had described Rose McBride, at her funeral Mass, as their 'golden Rose', and Margo sang 'Lady of Knock' with the line 'Golden Rose, Queen of Ireland', Father Creelman was again speaking about them both, this time at Tom's funeral Mass.

'Only eleven short weeks ago, I said at Rose's funeral that she would not like leaving Tom, as she was always at his side. Tom's favourite song was "Give My Love to Rose", and he was heartbroken to lose her. They are together again, side by side. Rose is smiling, and Tom is singing "Back in My Baby's Arms Again".

The celebrant went on to say that Tom and Rose were an example of a partnership that worked, in which each spouse cared for the other more than themselves. While Big Tom was the face and the voice that everyone saw and heard, Rose was in many ways the engine behind his success.

Rose and Tom in the early days of their marriage.

'He was a man big in stature, matched up with an even bigger heart. In the background, Rose was the grounding mechanism, the compass and the refuge needed for one of the most popular Irish country singing stars of our times.'

Rose and Tom's four children – Aisling, Siobhán, Thomas and Dermot – have been through an awful lot in the first four months of 2018, losing both of their parents within such a short time of each other. However, they were still willing to sit down and talk for this book about the parents they loved so well.

Aisling said that since she was a very young child, she remembers music sessions in their home – and she would sneak out of bed to see and hear the merriment and the sounds that emanated from the front room of the house.

'I remember lots of parties in the house, and it was a house that there was always plenty of craic in. There was always fun, and the parties went on to the wee small hours of the mornings.

'We had a large sitting room with a wooden floor, and we would sneak down and watch Daddy and Mammy and all their friends dancing, and we would think, wow! They knew how to live, how to enjoy themselves and have good fun.' Aisling enthused about how she watched, through a child's eyes, as her parents and their friends knocked sparks off that hardwood floor with their dancing – perhaps a half-set, or maybe jiving, to some of her dad's biggest hits.

'Sundays were always big days for people calling to our house. They would knock at the front door, and ask if Daddy was home or could they take photographs. Many times Daddy wasn't there, if he had been away working late the night before and the band might have stayed over in some hotel. Or if he had come home in the wee small hours, he might still be sleeping.

'Sundays were also football days in our house, and if Daddy was home, he would want us to have the dinner early so that we could go to a football match,' added Aisling.

At home with Rose and the children.

'Christmas was also a time when Daddy might have a little bit of down-time, and on Christmas nights there would always be a sing-song in the house. Different people would always be coming around for those gather-ings, and our home would always be full of people.

'On Christmas Eve, Mammy would always have to cook two hams, one for Christmas Eve and the other for Christmas Day. There were always so many of us around that those tasty hams would be attacked.' Aisling laughed as she recalled those happy Yuletide moments.

'On Christmas Eve, after Mass, everybody would gather in our house and the craic would go on till the wee small hours. Christmas night was party night, and then Dad would be gone off the next day to play somewhere with the band. On New Year's Eve too, I remember that he was always away work-ing, and we as a family would always sing "Auld Lang Syne" before he would leave. No matter how early he was leaving, we would gather in the living room and sing that before he went off to work,' she added.

In the more recent past, with the children grown up and with families of their own, the McBrides would sometimes celebrate the New Year in the home of one of the children, and Rose and Tom there with them.

'We could have a gathering in any of our homes then to ring in the New Year, with all of us together, as Daddy wasn't working at that stage in his life,' said Siobhán. She would, like the rest of them, sing along at the parties.

One of the songs Aisling sang, as Big Tom also told me in the interview in his home in 2004, was 'Far Side Banks Of Jordan'. While it was Aisling's singing of the song that influenced Tom to record it, Aisling says she never aspired to be a professional singer herself.

'I had been listening to Johnny Cash and June Carter singing it on a record, and I thought it was a lovely song. He liked the song too, and later on he decided to record it.

'The boys in our family sang more than us girls, and when we were grow-ing up, Thomas was a great drummer. He also used to sing a wee bit; one of the songs he liked to sing was, "Run to the Door".

'Siobhán and I usually just sang at the parties in the house,' says Aisling. 'We weren't ones for the limelight, but in the early years, when we had the pub in Castleblayney, the Monday nights were always big nights there. It was very busy, and we would always be there to gather glasses. Sometimes I would get up on stage with Daddy and sing a song or two.' For Aisling, those sessions in the Log Cabin pub were where her public singing career started and finished!

Aisling went on to university and qualified as a Science teacher, which is what she still does today. She is also busy rearing their three children with her husband Sean. Singing for her took a back seat to the daily work in the classroom and in the home.

'I just got stage fright regarding singing one night, and after that I wouldn't sing in the Log Cabin any more. I would panic if I was asked to sing, and would probably run to the bathroom and stay there till the requests for me to sing had passed over. That was the end of my singing career and I suppose, to quote the title of one of Daddy's songs, you could say that if I was asked to sing after that I would "Run to the Door",' laughed Aisling.

She also remembers how important Gaelic football was in the McBride household when they were growing up. Now it is important once again in Aisling's home, as her son Jason Duffy has already made the Armagh county team, at the age of twenty.

'He's a redhead, and so I think he takes after Daddy with his red hair, and he's a decent footballer too,' said Aisling. Was Big Tom proud of having a grandson on a county football team, albeit in the opposing county of Armagh? I asked.

'Oh! Sure, Daddy took everything in his stride. He wouldn't be boasting or blowing up somebody for what they were doing. He wasn't that type of man, but ach, I know that he was proud of Jason surely. However, he wouldn't have been shouting about it – that wasn't Dad's style,' she replied.

Aisling added that all her children 'tinkered' a bit with music in their early school-going years. 'But then when they reached their teens they all gave up the music – and as they were more interested in football, I suppose we just let them do so,' she said nonchalantly.

Meanwhile, Siobhán's young son Glen, who is only eleven, is also a keen footballer as well as being a singer and guitar player, like his granddad Tom. He has already been featured on RTÉ television – Glen sang and played guitar on 'You Are My Sunshine', along with his famous grandfather, on the 'Nationwide' special on Big Tom in the autumn of 2017.

'We were very proud of him doing that, as he had only started taking guitar lessons at the time. I manage a wee pre-school here in Oram, and Glen had done some lessons there, as well as getting a few tips from his granddad.

'It was suggested that, as Mary Kennedy was doing the TV programme on Daddy, it would be nice if some of the grandchildren were to play or sing a song. Glen gave it a go, and he did okay,' said his proud mum in her understated way. Siobhán added that when they were growing up, neither Tom or Rose McBride pushed them into learning music.

'We got piano lessons when we were young, but didn't take to those very well. We took little or no notice of Daddy playing music for a living in our early school-going years. It was only when Mammy took Aisling and me to a see him singing at a dance at the White Horse Inn in Cootehill, County Cavan, that I first saw him play before an audience,' she said.

On that occasion, Siobhan watched in awe and amazement as the crowd rose to their feet and took to the floor to dance the night away as soon as her dad and the band started to play.

'All those people were out dancing, and many of them were standing in front of the stage looking up at Daddy and the band, and I was thinking to myself, "Why are all those people doing that?" I couldn't understand it. We went to the bathroom at one stage, and as kids of only ten or eleven, we were also amazed to hear others saying, "Oh my God! Isn't Big Tom great?" or, "Isn't there a great crowd?" or, "He's a great singer." As that was my first time hearing all that, I was still thinking to myself, "Oh my good-ness! That's my father they're talking about." It was my first realisation that Daddy was famous.'

Talking to the four children of Big Tom and Rose McBride today, it is obvious that they were brought up in a very ordinary household, away from the spotlight and any trappings of success, and were encouraged to have a strong work ethic in life. That is still apparent in all of them today. Siobhán and her husband Austin encourage that same work ethic in their own children, as do Aisling and John, Thomas and Rita and Dermot and Rita. For example, Dermot McBride had only come in that evening from driving a truck to and from Dublin when he met me to do an interview for this book about his late parents. Then, straight afterwards, he had to go out to feed the cattle in the field beside Siobhán's house. Only after tending to the livestock did he go home for his dinner – no pampered son of a superstar about that!

Together at home: Rose and Tom in more recent times. At the back, from left to right, are Thomas, Aisling, Siobhan and Dermot.

The same is true of Thomas. He was heading off to Scotland early on the morning after our interview to work, driving a piece of plant machinery for the well-known pipe-laying and construction firm John Murphy Ltd.

'I'm working in Inverness at present. I like Scotland, and so did Daddy. He even thought about moving there way back in the early 1970s, when he saw a place there that he liked. He was going to move the whole family there, but Mammy put the brakes on,' laughs Thomas.

'That time it was only a wee cottage that we lived in here in Oram. While we had plans to build a new house in the field above where our present house now stands, we eventually decided to stay where we were, and Daddy built on the extension to the cottage.'

The girls also share this same work ethic that seems to permeate the McBride households. Aisling and Siobhán McBride have always been busy with their careers – Aisling teaching Science in a school in County Armagh, while Siobhan manages the pre-school in Oram.

'I went into the childcare business, which is tough enough, but it is a very rewarding job. We opened a wee pre-school just down the road here in the community centre in 2009, and I manage that.'

Their dad and mum kept them all grounded growing up. While Big Tom was never very strict on his children, he didn't have to be, as he was away so much anyway. While Rose had to be more strict, she was also fair to them all, according to Siobhán.

'Daddy never gave out to us, even though I'm sure there were times when he could have had reason to give out to us. But Mammy took care of that business, and Daddy would never raise his voice. He was so gentle and kind, as they both were, but in his case he never disciplined us at all,' said Siobhán.

Both she and Aisling say that they always loved when he came back from touring in England, as there would be presents for all of the four children.

'Either Mammy would phone him, or else he would phone home, and we children would always get a chance to chat with him. Our first question would be, "When are you coming home, Daddy?" and the second question would be, "What are you going to bring me home?"

'He would always shop for us when in England, or in the duty free on the way home, and bring back bottles of perfume or bits of jewellery for Aisling and myself, and something else for the lads. He would never come back from England without bringing something home to each of us – we would be searching through his case to see what was in it for us as soon as he came back,' added Siobhán.

'At the memorial Mass for Dad, a man came up to me and said that he played football with Dad, and sat beside him during their schooldays. I just had to ask that man to tell me what Daddy was like at school. I never remember Daddy talking much about being at school, and so many say that he was never there much anyway!

'But this man told me that they shared the same desk, and whenever Dad did come to school, the first thing he would say was "give me a look at your homework". He would take that man's homework and look at it, so that he could do his own. That man told me that my daddy lived for break-time in school. "Once the bell rang, he would just grab a football and was out in the yard. I think he just came to school to play football at break-time," said that man. I replied that it reminded me of my own son Glen, as I think he only goes to school to play football too, during break-time,' she laughed.

Like his granddad Tom, Glen's uncles Dermot and Thomas have always loved playing or watching football games, as Thomas explains:

'I played a good bit of football in younger years. But I was always very injury-prone. I broke my ankle twice, and before anybody told me to stop playing, I stopped doing so myself.

'At eighteen, I was playing with a great bunch of lads, and we won the minor championship with Oram, but after that I didn't play much football. I was more into working on diggers and other machinery. Dermot, like our dad, did spells with the county team, but like Dad as well, he was also playing music at that time. He hadn't the time to devote to doing enough training with either the club team or the county,' says Thomas. His eldest son Stephen (twenty-nine) is also a talented footballer.

Big Tom and Tall Tom: Tom and Thomas Junior at home.

Thomas also relates a humorous memory about when he first played professionally, as a stand-in drummer in his dad's band in Dublin:

'It was a privilege to play in Dad's band. The reason I got the job was because the drummer at that time had taken ill. I was playing in a small pub band back then. There were four of us in that group; all of us were cousins. Daddy asked me if I was fit for the job in The Travellers while the drummer was off sick, and I said I'd give it a try.

'Our first gig was on a Thursday night, in Barry's Hotel in Dublin. I was very nervous, especially when I looked out and saw that the place was jammed with dancers. Daddy said to me, "If you see me making a sign with my hand, similar to pulling a car handbrake, then pull her up, as you're going too fast." So I was watching Daddy's hands all the time to see was I going too fast or too slow. The pressure was on me that night,' laughed Thomas.

Looking back on his stint in his father's band, he says they were 'great times', and he has great memories of the people that he met.

'Many of Daddy's fans were like family, and he would spend as much time talking to them after the gig as he would singing on stage. That's the way Dad was. The boys would be waiting in the car to go home, but he wouldn't go till the last fan had left the hall. He opened his heart to everybody, and he listened to every story. Daddy had serious patience, and he was witty too – he could knock you down with one-liners. He had a wonderful way with words – he was quick-witted.'

Thomas was asked to do some music management work with a young singer from Newry a few years ago, but it 'just didn't work out for the lad'. 'You need to get a lucky break in this business, and unfortunately this young lad didn't get the break, and it didn't work out for him.' Thomas was also road manager for singer Jimmy Buckley for four years.

'I worked for Jimmy, driving to the gigs with the gear and setting it up, as well as looking after the merchandise. While I wouldn't have met as many people as I would have met at Daddy's dances, I would still have met a good cross-section of them. Jimmy Buckley is a good country singer. Similar to my dad, he would have sang his songs from the heart, and I enjoyed my four years working with him,' says Thomas.

Like his dad, Thomas McBride is quick-witted too. When one of his sisters remarked that she remembers him singing 'Run to the Door', he laughed loudly and responded by saying that if so, 'it was after the National Anthem had been played and the show was over'!

'But I dabbled a wee bit in the singing and playing, and am sorry now that I didn't spend more time at it when younger. Especially when we had the wee band with my cousins – Jerome, who plays with Declan Nerney's band now; Peter Brady, another cousin of ours; as well as Margaret Murray, who is also a cousin, and whose brother Brendan Murray worked with Daddy in the bands as a road manager for about eighteen years.

'When I was in that group, I had started singing a few songs, but when I heard myself back I didn't like what I was hearing. So if I didn't like what I was hearing from my own voice, then I don't think that anyone else would have liked it either,' laughed Thomas.

Thomas's eldest son Stephen showed some interest in country music in his teenage years. Big Tom told me in the 2004 interview that he was surprised to be told by his grandson that some of the CDs he was playing in his room at that time, when he was only fourteen, were 'Big Tom CDs'. His granddad remarked that 'disco might take over' young Stephen's music tastes after a while. But it wasn't so much disco as football that lured him away from the singing. The last family wedding that Big Tom attended, only a few weeks before he passed away, was Stephen's wedding, and Thomas says that his dad was 'only able to go to the church part of the ceremony'.

'Dad was too weak to go to the wedding reception, but it was still great to see him go to that much of it. He went back to the house afterwards and had photos taken with the newly married couple, which was lovely,' added Thomas.

Rose had hoped to be at the wedding of her grandson too, and had all the arrangements made to be there. But sadly, she passed away only a few weeks earlier. But Rose had insisted that all the family be together when Mary Kennedy and the camera crew from RTÉ came to Oram to film the special programme on Tom in 2017.

'We were all pushed into singing for the "Nationwide" TV programme, but Dermot is the singer in our family – he does a lot of singing and playing with The Outlaws group. He was with Daddy in the band since he was sixteen, first working as a roadie, and then he took up playing the bass guitar. There was a slot for him in the band from time to time, as other musicians were moving on. He is the farmer in the family too, which is another tough business to be in at present,' said Thomas.

The youngest son of Tom and Rose McBride, the lanky Dermot, who stands at well over six feet tall, is, like his father was, shy, bashful and retiring about his ability to sing and play guitar.

'I was doing the gear in the band for maybe eight or ten years with The Travellers, and then with The Mainliners. They re-formed in 1989, and they played, on and off, for seven or eight years, before some of them started to drift off. Perhaps they had enough of the business. Firstly, when Ginger decided to take a break I was playing a bit of rhythm guitar at sessions in our house, and my father suggested I play it, or else the bass, in the band for some of the dates.

'It was later on that they started to get me to sing a song or two as well. But I'd always have some excuse not to sing – I would say that I had a sore throat, or make up some other excuse. I was very nervous about singing on stage at that time. A half an hour before I would be due to sing, I would be trying to remember the words, and it would be panic time for me. I don't know why this panic would set in, but I suppose that I'm more confident now when working with the group The Outlaws,' says Dermot.

He says that as a child growing up, it was when he saw people calling to their home to get photographs, and when he saw his dad 'on a few TV shows' that he realised that he was famous. But Dermot also said that as his father 'never passed any remarks about anything like that', the family just accepted him as going out to do another job.

However, Dermot soon discovered that when he was on the road himself with the band, and travelling all over the country, it was almost impossible to continue training with the Monaghan senior football team, or even with the local club on a regular basis.

Unassumingly, he makes light of his time wearing the county colours on the football field.

'Ah! Sure I pulled on the county jersey a few times all right. But the training, even for the younger boys, was mostly on Friday nights, and that was never suitable when I was in the band – it would have been the same probably in my father's time.

'I also played mostly at midfield for the Oram club, and I was involved in the backroom team with the Senior side, along with many other people, just helping them out, as well as with some of the under-age teams,' said Dermot. He talked to me in the kitchen of his sister's home at 6pm, just after coming home from a day of truck driving that had started for him at 8am.

'For years, I would take himself to the football matches. During the last few years, his walking wasn't so good, and some people would kindly give us passes so that we could get him closer to the action.

'He really enjoyed going to those matches if the weather was good at all. My own young boy plays a bit of football as well now, and it's nice to see that he has an interest in the game,' says Dermot.

Does he intend to go on singing and playing? I asked. 'Well, I like to do a bit, but I couldn't see it as a full-time career. Maybe sometime I'll do a bit of recording, but it's not top of the list for me. I probably had a few chances in the past, and I didn't jump at them, as it never really appealed to me that much. There is always a lot to be done on the farm, or else truck driving, but somehow we get around it all.

'I have great memories from playing in the band with Dad. Anyone that ever worked with him would say he was easy to play beside on any stage. He wouldn't be giving out about anything, and he would just be glad that you were playing.

Big Tom The Travellers

'One memory that I have from the early days, when we had the Log Cabin pub – a wee group came to play, but one of them got nervous about missing notes, and he sat down and wasn't going to play. My father came over to him and said to just give it a go, and play away as best you can – he encouraged him,' added Dermot.

When our interview was over, Dermot headed to one of his farm fields to give the cattle some silage and fill the water troughs – no pretentions about being the son of a famous singer there.

While Big Tom and Rose leave a great legacy of hard work, love of family and appreciation for music among their four children, they were also extremely proud of their nine grandchildren.

Thomas and Rita have two: Stephen, who is the eldest grandchild at twenty-nine, and Amy, who is twenty-four. Aisling and Sean have three boys, the Armagh footballer Jason the eldest at twenty, Conor (seventeen) and Gavan (fifteen). Dermot and Rita have two children: Ciaran (thirteen) and Amelia (six). Finally, Siobhán's young footballer, and the singer of 'You Are My Sunshine' on television, is Glen Forde, who is eleven, while his younger sister Alisha is six. Suffice to say that they are all part of the great McBride legacy.

MAINLINERS—BIG TOM Reading His Fan Mail

Hit Records - OLD LOG CABIN FOR SALE and GENTLE MOTHER

Chapter 8

Travelling On

In 1975, as his career fronting The Mainliners was flying, Big Tom dropped a bombshell on the Irish music scene. He announced that it was time for him to travel on. He was creating a new band, The Travellers.

At this time, the crowds at his dances were massive. Even a man who Tom admired on the international music scene, Mick Jagger, was alleged to have come up to him looking for an autograph! The change of band was to bring many new challenges for Tom, and unknown to him, he was to record on equipment supplied by international business impresario Richard Branson.

Tom McBride was a man of few words. Especially in his younger years, perhaps he let his songs and music do the talking. While his words about splitting with The Mainliners were not many, and were measured, the media made up for that with lots of speculation in the press even before it happened.

If one was to use more scientific terms, perhaps the decision could be described as a seismic shift on the showband scene in Ireland at that time. Even to family members such as his brother-in-law Paddy King, who was to be in the new band, the news, when Tom told him, came as a surprise. But reports in the press were suggesting that Robert Irwin, Paddy's colleague in The Everglades and later Tom's manager, had hoped that it might happen.

In an issue of the *Evening Press* in early 1975, a report stated that 'John McCormick, manager of Big Tom and The Mainliners, hasn't come across with any official info yet.

'Last weekend there appeared many rumours and speculative stories in the Sunday nationals. However I feel that the true and full story about the Big Tom saga has yet to emerge,' stated the story.

Another newspaper report, a few months earlier, had stated that there were rumours that Big Tom was going to sign a contract with 'a top ranking promoter' in his home town. As the late Tony Loughman operated the Top Rank music agency in the town, this report was very pointed indeed. But he did move to Top Rank Entertainment later on, after the split happened. Big Tom and his new band, The Travellers, stayed with John McCormick initially, for approximately one year. During this time, John continued managing The Mainliners and their new lead singer, John Hanratty from Crossmaglen, whose stage name was John Glenn.

Both bands continued to record in Castle Studios, Castleblayney. The studio manager there was Robert Irwin of The Everglades, who was later a drummer and manager with The Travellers. He talks about the Richard Branson, and even a possible Mick Jagger, link with Tom later on in this chapter.

The magazine that was the bible of the national music industry in Ireland at that time, *New Spotlight*, devoted pages to the split up of Big Tom and The Mainliners. The article, titled 'The Partin' of the Ways', was written by Paschal Mooney, who later went on to great fame as an RTÉ radio and television presenter of country music programmes. Paschal Mooney eventually became a Senator in Seanad Éireann.

'Last week's shock announcement that Big Tom was parting company with The Mainliners, his band of ten years, came after months of speculation that "the big fella" was considering a move,' wrote Paschal.

'Big Tom and The Mainliners have achieved every possible accolade in the business. Every one of their singles have been Top 10, Top 5 or Number 1 (three of them). Their LPs (almost half a dozen to date) have sold in vast quantities. Their *Ashes of Love* LP has sold over 100,000 in six months while box office records have tumbled everywhere,' stated Paschal's report.

In a separate, two-page feature, also written by Paschal, *New Spotlight* sent photographer Liam Quigley to Castleblayney to get photographs of the two bands rehearsing. John Glenn and The Mainliners were rehearsing in Castle Studios, while Big Tom and The Travellers were rehearsing in Oram National School.

'The local school is very handy for us for rehearsals,' said Tom, while Mainliners bandleader Henry McMahon was also 'full of confidence that their new vocalist, John Glenn, would prove to be a popular figure in the ballrooms', according to the report.

Paschal Mooney's story went on to state that 'The Everglades (sorry The Travellers) are blending in well with the gentle giant … "Well he hasn't said too much so far," reports Paddy King, who plays bass with The Travellers.

'As Big Tom, even at his happiest, never says too much, I wouldn't be too worried about that,' added Paschal Mooney's report.

When interviewed for this book, Paddy King said he was shocked on the night that he came home and Big Tom told him that he was splitting from The Mainliners. 'I had come home from a gig with The Everglades when Tom, and one of his biggest fans, the late Johnny Brown, were in the kitchen at home. I came in the door, and Tom said to me that he was leaving The Mainliners.

'It came as such a shock, and I said to him, "Why would you do that?" But he replied they had done all they could over the years together, and they had nothing more left to achieve. His next words were, "We want your band." I should have been over the moon, but I felt it was madness, as The Mainliners were huge at the time,' adds Paddy.

Paddy King remembers his own first forays into the music business. 'I started playing with two others in a wee group. Because I was in the band, the other lads probably knew that we would get some work playing as support act to Big Tom and The Mainliners. At the time I was working in a shoe factory, and getting £2.50 a week. The first night we got a gig with Tom it was on a Thursday in the Pavesi Ballroom in Donegal. I was standing on the stage trying to play the bass – many of my friends will say that I'm still trying to play it,' laughs Paddy.

He says he 'had a big red face', and was 'petrified', as the place was packed with 'as many as 1,500 or 1,600 people'. When Tom came out on stage, 'the screaming and roaring of the fans' was amazing, as 'Gentle Mother' was a big hit at that time.

'When we got back home that night, as I was getting out of the car, Tom handed me some money and when I went into the house, it was £5. That

was a fortune in those times. It was double the wages that I had been getting for working a full week in the shoe factory. So I said "music is for me"
after that, if I could earn that sort of money for a few hours' work.'

Paddy went on to play and sing with a band called The Everglades for
a number of years. Then one night, his brother-in-law Big Tom suggested
that he and the rest of that group should consider becoming his new band,
The Travellers. It was shock news from Big Tom, even for his brother-in-
law to hear.

He also says that because he was the brother-in-law of Big Tom, he was
the one that was seen as having encouraged him to leave The Mainliners,
when in fact this was not the situation at all.

McCooey, Big Tom, Paddy King and Harry Conlon of The Travellers, performing at the 1976
Herald Pop Poll Concert.

'He had the new name, The Travellers, already picked. But, of course, I got blamed for splitting up Big Tom and The Mainliners, when in fact I told him not to do so. Anyway, our former band, The Everglades, suddenly went from being a middle-of-the-road act to be right up there at the top. On our first night in Athy, a ballroom that had been closed for five years, and they couldn't fit in the entire crowd – there was about 2,500 people there.'

Before he left The Mainliners, Big Tom recorded one final vinyl LP with them, titled *Souvenirs*. In an interview, again with *New Spotlight* magazine, he said it was the best he had ever done up to that point.

'I've used some of The Mainliners on the session. But I also asked people such as Paddy Cole on sax, Shelly (then lead singer with Big Valley), Ray Moore on trumpet (from the Paddy Cole band) and Jim Bradley (piano player with Brian Coll's band) to help out, so it should be popular,' said Tom.

Big Tom was right, as the *Souvenirs* album became another best-seller. It also included one of his most popular songs, 'Run To The Door'. Even with the young dancers of today, that songs remains popular, and it has been covered in recent times by new country star Derek Ryan.

The *Souvenirs* album is an eclectic selection of country songs. It includes the sad story of the around-the-world lady pilot known as the First Lady of the Air, Amelia Earhart. Her plane 'came down in shark-infested waters in the blue Pacific Ocean far away', to quote from the song. The album also had a fine rendition of 'The Year That Clayton Delaney Died', written by the man known as 'the storyteller' of country music in the US, Tom T Hall. Years later, when Tom T toured in Ireland, he and Big Tom got together socially and they shared more than a few whiskeys, according to informed sources.

Songs with a mother theme were also included on this LP, such as 'Mama's Roses', 'I Have An Aged Mother' and 'Rock My Cradle Once Again'. But

Big Tom also delved into the more progressive side of country with his rendition of the Crosby, Stills, Nash and Young song 'Teach Your Children'. This was later released as a single by him in the UK, but with only limited success.

But perhaps one of the most controversial songs on the album is a Conway Twitty hit, which had originally been banned by some radio stations in the US. It was titled 'You've Never Been This Far Before'. This was a song about two lovers exploring their bodies for the first time. While it caused controversy

Big Tom accepts his award as Top Irish Country Singer at the Tuam Herald Pop Poll Awards show from author Tom Gilmore at a concert in St Jarlath's College Hall, Tuam in 1976.

in the States, its lyrics seemed to go largely unnoticed by country music fans in Ireland. They simply regarded it as a good country song with a strong dancing beat, especially the way Tom had recorded it, with lots of brass instruments in the backing.

If the controversial lyrics went largely unnoticed by the fans, this was not the situation in his own home, as Big Tom explained to me during the interview with him in 2004.

'I thought that my wife would kill me when she heard the words of that song – it certainly didn't go down well with her when Rose listened to that track. But we got over that too,' said Tom with a smile.

Rose was a very religious woman all her life, but in a quiet way. To quote her local priest, Father Leo Creelman, at her funeral Mass, she 'treated her local church in the same way that she treated her own home'.

The priest went on to say that she arranged the flowers for the church in Oram regularly, and also ironed the altar clothes to perfection.

'I remember one time that she was upset when she noticed, after the other items were placed on the altar, that there was a crease in part of the cloth.

'As there wasn't time to remove the cloth, and all the other items that were placed on it, to re-iron it, Rose rushed up the road to her home and got the iron and ironed out the crease there on the altar,' said Father Creelman.

Indeed, on the day she was laid to rest, I was saying goodbye to Big Tom in the church in Oram, and I remarked on how great a person Rose was for everybody. Tom replied, 'Above all else, Rose was a brilliant Catholic,' with tears welling up in his eyes.

So one could imagine that in the more conservative Ireland of 1975, she wasn't too enamoured with her husband singing such a song, with what would then have been seen as sexually suggestive lyrics.

Anyway, there was no controversy at all among music lovers. The Souvenirs album seemed to go down well with fans of both his old band, The Mainliners, and his new group, The Travellers.

Writing in one of the Sunday newspapers in 1976, Bill Stuart stated that Big Tom had revealed to him that things had not been going well between himself and The Mainliners 'for a full year past'.

'It all came to a head in March last year,' he said. 'Things were getting sour and stale with The Mainliners. We had done everything we were going to do and we got more or less careless.

'It was that simple that we had taken it for granted. I was even contemplating leaving the business altogether,' said Tom.

According to the report, it was at that time that he got an offer from Top Rank Entertainments.

'I didn't even consider it at the time. But then I thought about it again, and I thought that maybe if I did make a change, then I'd maybe take a new interest in the game for another few years.'

The report goes on to state that Tom worried a lot while deciding what to do. 'It's hard to go your own way after going on for ten years with fellows that you know. I thought for three weeks before I left those boys and I'd safely say there were nights I didn't sleep a wink.

'I always hold The Mainliners in high regard. They were one of the main reasons for my success and you don't forget things like that,' said Tom.

'But The Mainliners and me weren't going to last forever. It was going to happen someday anyway.'

Initially, both bands continued to be managed by John McCormick, but the alliance wasn't working out. While Tom said 'there was no quarrel about money', he was unhappy about the level of promotion that they were getting. So when the year's contract was up, Tom and The Travellers moved on to Top Rank Entertainments. Here they were managed by Robert Irwin, who was also manager of Castle Studios in Castleblayney, where both bands were recording.

Indeed it was while Robert was a drummer with The Everglades that he and the lads cobbled together enough money to buy recording studio equipment in the UK and set up Castle Studios, which later became Big Tom's Studio.

A fault on a recording that they had made in a Dublin studio convinced Robert that he should start a recording studio himself in Castleblayney.

'I found out that there was a sixteen-track Ampex machine for sale in a place called The Manor Studio in Oxford. I phoned up and done the deal, and asked the lads if they would join me in getting the price of the machine.

'I even borrowed £300 from my mother, and I told her I would pay it back with interest in twelve months. She did without hesitation, and I did pay her back as promised. So we gathered all the money that we had between us, and off we went to Oxford to buy the machine,' says Robert.

'It was a state-of-the-art machine, as there was no other sixteen-track machine in the country at that time. The Manor Studio was in an old-style English manor house, and I paid the £4,500 in sterling – fivers, tenners, pound notes. As it was a lot of money in 1973, I said to the man who I was paying that in Ireland we had a tradition of getting a "luck penny" when we bought items.

'He said he "never heard of that one before". But he made a phone call to a fellow called Richard, and told him that "the guys from Ireland had paid the money, but were looking for a luck penny".

'When he put down the phone, he said that "Richard on the other end of the phone said to give ye twenty quid luck penny", which he did. I asked him who was he talking to, and he replied he was talking to Richard Branson, who owned Virgin Records and he also owned The Manor Studio.'

Robert was surprised when he heard that, and he was even more surprised to learn that Mike Oldfield's Tubular Bells album had been recorded on the machine that they had bought. 'We got steel guitarist Basil Hendricks to put the studio together, and Big Tom was the first man through the door to record with us,' added Robert.

'We recorded the RTÉ Light Orchestra, Philomena Begley, Ray Lynam, Susan McCann, Brian Coll, Hugo Duncan, traditional fiddle player Sean Maguire, and our own records with The Everglades, plus many others in the studio, beside the Lyric Theatre'.

Eventually, in 1976, they sold the equipment to Big Tom and Tony Loughman, and that's how it moved to Tony's Top Rank premises, when it became known as Big Tom's Studio. It was very successful here for years afterwards. Most of Big Tom's records with The Travellers were recorded there, as well as the song that launched the career of Daniel O'Donnell, 'My Donegal Shore'.

Robert became manager of Big Tom and The Travellers on 1 January 1976, and he was there until 1981, when he left to pursue his many other business interests. He is still an entrepreneur, and owns Irwin's Tiles & Hardwood Flooring in Castleblayney.

Kevin McCooey, who was a member of The Travellers during those years, went on to manage Big Tom right up to the end. He has wonderful memories of what was a close friendship as well as a great business relationship.

'I worked with Tom for forty-three years. He gave me a job, and I will be ever grateful for that. He was a kind person, and a fun person to be around,' said Kevin, who suggested many of the songs that Tom chose to include on albums with The Travellers. The first of these was titled *When the Roses Bloom Again*.

It was appropriate that their second album should be titled *Travel On*, as it travelled all the way to number one in the Irish pop albums chart. Their next album, *I Would Like to See You Again*, was also a massive chart success. But when Tom went to Nashville to record the *Blue Wings* album in 1980, it did not turn out to be the commercial success that he had hoped for. His fear of flying resulted in Tom, and his songwriter friend Johnny McCauley, travelling to New York by ship. They went across the USA by Greyhound bus to make his only Nashville album. While regarded by many as one of his best albums, *Blue Wings* failed to set the charts alight.

'Johnny asked me if I would like to go to Nashville, and while I said I would love to do so, there was no way that I was going to fly there. This was a strange fear that I got, because in the early days I didn't mind flying. We would fly back and over to England just for one show on a Saturday, and be back to play some venue in Ireland on the Sunday, and I didn't mind flying at that time,' Tom told Shay Healy in the RTÉ television programme 'A Little Bit Country', which was screened in 2006.

During his days with The Mainliners, even the lure of a massive fee for playing one night in New York couldn't entice Tom to fly, according to a story in the Sunday Independent in 1974.

'The latest staggering offer came a short time back when New York's top promoters, Bill Hartigan and Tim Moynehan, cabled manager John McCormick an offer of $7,500 for one show by Big Tom. They wanted him to top the bill in Madison Square Garden on St Patrick's Night,' stated the report.

It added that in New York and Boston, where his records sold in large quantities, it was a pity that Big Tom's many fans would not get the opportunity to see Ireland's top attraction.

'However, there's hope, for John McCormick is presently negotiating with a shipping company, with a view to taking the band to America sometime in 1975 by sea.

'When that day comes the docks of New York will probably be painted green to welcome Ireland's most popular singing ambassador,' stated the report.

That day was ultimately never to happen. By 1975, John McCormick had other, more pressing issues to deal with in Ireland, as Big Tom was splitting from The Mainliners. But even with his new band, The Travellers, Tom was not travelling to gigs by air.

He went into greater detail, in an interview with his friend Michael Commins, about what caused his fear of flying in the first instance. That was for Michael's programme on Irish television a few years ago, which was also shown again in 2018 on Keep It Country TV.

Tom said that a fire in one of the engines forced the pilot to abort a flight that he was on in London. When they got back to the runway, 'there were fire engines and ambulances everywhere and they were all waiting for us,' which Tom said scared the life out of him.

He said that they finally left for Dublin on another flight, and he was given a magazine to read to help calm his fears during that flight. 'But if anyone asked me what did I read, I couldn't tell them, as all I did was look at the headings and the photos,' said Tom.

However, in 1972, while he was with The Mainliners, Tom had to break his vow never to fly again. He was forced to do so when his father, Samuel, died suddenly on 10 November that year.

According to a report in *New Spotlight* magazine, Big Tom was on stage at a 'crowded Carousel Club in Camden Town when he was told of his father's sudden death'.

'He went to his dressing room immediately and Henry McMahon told the rest of The Mainliners. They decided to return to Ireland with Big Tom as soon as possible. By 3am travel arrangements were confirmed and Big Tom and three of The Mainliners later left Heathrow Airport for home,' stated the report.

He took slower modes of transportation in 1980, travelling by boat and train to London to meet Johnny McCauley for their trip to a recording studio in Nashville.

'When going to Nashville, I went to London first, and from there with Johnny to Southampton. We boarded the *QE2* ship, which took five days to make the trip to New York. It was rough enough one night on board the *QE2* also. We were tossed around a bit, and had to be holding on to the curtains that night,' laughed Tom.

After staying in New York for a few days, they got on a Greyhound bus for the trip across the country.

'You often hear about Greyhound buses in country songs, and I thought they were a luxury coach. But at that time, the one we were on for twenty-three hours, from New York to Nashville, wasn't luxurious,' said Tom.

'It was my first Irish album that contained all originals [all written by Johnny McCauley], and the Nashville sound on it was different. We often said afterwards that if it had been recorded in Ireland, it would have been a bigger hit at the time, as it would have a more Irish flavour to the backing. It had the American flavour, and while the backing was well done, you would know that it was different from the way it would have been recorded in Ireland. Sometimes we regretted afterwards that we didn't do it in Ireland,' said Tom.

'He always said that if he had recorded those songs in Ireland he would have had at least two more big hits,' says Kevin McCooey. 'He was right, because Daniel O'Donnell recorded "My Donegal Shore" later in Tom's studio. Several other singers had hits with "Where The Grass Grows The Greenest" – both taken from Tom's Nashville album.'

'Tom was the first artist ever to go to Nashville from Ireland with a full album of all original songs,' Kevin adds.

But irrespective of what way that Nashville record went in the charts, the crowds at the dances remained massive everywhere that Big Tom and The Travellers played.

Above and below: En route to Nashville, by cruise liner and Greyhound bus.

Paddy King says that the band's popularity remained huge and constant at dances all over Ireland and in the UK. Then, in 1981, 'Four Country Roads' became such a popular hit that almost every radio programme in the country had to play it.

Like many others major hits – including, in a very different music genre, 'Whiskey In The Jar' for Thin Lizzy – Paddy King believes that the distinctive guitar riff played by band member Thomas Kiernan on 'Four Country Roads' also contributed enormously to its success.

'That guitar riff that Thomas Kiernan did at the start of the song will live on forever. It's one of the great guitar licks of country music in Ireland. I think we were somewhere in Offaly or Laois on the night we were rehearsing the song when Thomas came up with this guitar lick, and it was magic.

'Johnny McCauley was a great songwriter, and every town has four roads. It didn't matter if you were from Castleblayney or Castlebar, if you were in a foreign land that song brought you home, as did "Back To Castleblayney". Both Tom and Johnny McCauley knew the four roads and almost every blade of grass in Glenamaddy so well that they put real feeling into every word of that song. It was written and sung from the heart, and could have been about any town in Ireland,' added Paddy.

Michael Commins, Tom's life-long friend and colleague, later said, 'Tom always said, if you don't have a feel for the song, then don't sing it. Too many people nowadays sing country music, but they don't feel it, and it doesn't come across.'

That dovetailed neatly with something that Big Tom told me in the interview at his home in Oram in 2004. 'People often send me songs and say they might suit my style. I listen to them, but if I can't put feeling into a song, I won't sing it,' said Tom back then.

* * *

Like a reaper's scythe cutting a swathe through fields of corn, the headlights of myriad Morris Minors, Minis, Volkswagen Beetles, buses and other vehicles on Saturday nights cut paths through the four dark roads to Glenamaddy, on their way to the Sound of Music club. The venue was operated by a doyen of dancehall promoters, the late Joe O'Neill, throughout the 1960s, 1970s and 1980s.

Joe passed away over six years before Big Tom, and shortly after his great friend, London-based singer-songwriter Johnny McCauley. Johnny was inspired to write the hit 'Four Country Roads' by Joe's ballroom and sadly he has also moved on to sing and compose songs for the heavenly choirs. Now that trio are together again in that ballroom in the sky.

'Once in a while I hear the Sound of Music in the winter nights,' states a line from the song about the four country roads that lead to Glenamaddy. Without the Sound of Music dancehall, or its dedicated owner Joe O'Neill, that song might never have been written or have become a hit for Big Tom.

But while Big Tom might have been high in the charts with 'Four Country Roads', he indicated quite firmly, one evening in Glenamaddy, that he had no wish to fly high over the town to see those four roads made famous by him from the air. 'No way am I going up on that little plane,' he said, to his friend, dancehall owner and pilot Joe O'Neill, to his band mate Kevin McCooey and to this writer, as we took to the air to see the 'Four Country Roads' from above!

Tom was a man who had his feet planted firmly on the ground, both as a singer and as a person, according to Kevin McCooey. Kevin added that it was only in the later years that 'the establishment, and particularly RTÉ, realised that he was a unique and a special talent'.

'As a singer he had a great range, and I think one song that really shows up his range is the track 'Wall Of Loneliness' on the *Souvenirs* album. There is a massive range on that song, and he hits it as clean as a whistle.

'Tom was progressive in his choice of songs from way back then. He was doing stuff by Kristofferson, Waylon Jennings or Conway Twitty from the early days. He was also one of the first to do gospel songs, including "One Day at A Time" on the *Travel On* album in 1977. That was almost a year before Gloria and others made it a hit on this side of the Atlantic,' added Kevin.

Kevin was in The Travellers when they played to the biggest crowd that Big Tom ever entertained. That was at the London Irish Festival in Roundwood Park, Willesden Green, London. 'There were 82,000 people there that day, and it was an electric atmosphere when Tom took to the stage,' says Kevin.

But according to Tom's friend, and former football team mate from teenage years, Carl Laverty, the big man was as happy playing to a small group as he was to a big crowd.

'Tom was as happy singing to fifty senior citizens at our local Christmas party, or in a local shed at Shannon's Thresher where the corn would be threshed, like in the old days, and where there would only be a few people,' says Carl.

But none of those friends and family members could confirm or deny rumours that Big Tom may once have signed an autograph for Mick Jagger.

In reality, it seems unlikely – in 1991, when Tom was asked who was the person that he would most like to meet, in the book *The A to Z of Irish Country Stars* by Brian Carthy, his reply was Mick Jagger. Yet the June 1988 issue of *Magill* magazine published a report alleging that the two had met by chance, in a bar in Castleblayney.

The report claimed that Jagger liked Ireland, because no one here seemed to recognise him.

'He walked freely around the highways and byways of Monaghan, weekend after weekend, without attracting as much as a single autograph hunter,' stated the story.

But one evening, when standing at a bar in a hotel in Castleblayney, he allegedly saw a group of young women looking in his direction and whispering among themselves.

Then, when 'they suddenly ran across the floor in his direction', he was doubly surprised to discover that he was not the object of their attention at all. Rather, it was a big man, 'built like the side of a house', who was standing right behind him at the bar.

The report goes on to quote Jagger as saying to a companion, 'Who the fack's that?' He was told that it was a country singer named Big Tom, who was 'a big star in these parts'.

'"I must get his facking autograph," declared the Rolling One.

'When the crowd of females had dispersed, Jagger sauntered up to Tom, stuck a piece of paper under his nose and demanded his autograph,' stated the *Magill* report.

'"Who'll I make it out to?" enquired the Big Fellow.

'"Mick Jagger, man," replied the rubber-lipped one, rather nonplussed and not a little miffed.

'Big Tom studied him carefully for a while. "Aye," he pronounced finally, "and you look like him too."'

Well, so the *Magill* magazine story goes.

Did this encounter involving the two big stars from very different music genres ever happen? One would have to imagine that it's most unlikely, especially if Big Tom still had a wish to meet Mick Jagger three years later, as it says in Brian Carthy's book.

However, Robert Irwin says that while it's unlikely, it's still possible that this meeting might have happened.

'When Tom would say something like that, it meant he wasn't sure, and he thought that somebody might be acting the rascal – but he wasn't sure.

'Mick Jagger was often a visitor at Castle Leslie in Glaslough, County Monaghan, around that time. So I suppose it's possible that he could have been in a pub in Castleblayney too when Big Tom was also there. But the only person that can answer that now is Mick Jagger,' concluded Robert Irwin with a laugh.

Chapter 9

Big Tom's Kingdom

Visiting the home of a King in Ireland became a frequent occurrence for many fans of Big Tom, who became his friends over the years. But when Tom himself went visiting in the early days of his career, to give his first media interview in 1967, he went almost undercover to do so. The interview was conducted in a monastery, and the student priest who interviewed him, Father Brian D'Arcy, risked being thrown out of his order for doing it. In fact, the interview had to be published under a false name!

But for the McBride children – Thomas Junior, Siobhán, Aisling and Dermot – growing up in the home of a King was not much different to living in any other home in rural Ireland. Perhaps the main difference was the frequency of visits by fans, calling to say hello to their famous father. Many had their photos taken, either with him or beside the wrought-iron gate, emblazoned with the words 'Big Tom' in metal lettering, accompanied by two (heavy metal!) guitars, all made by a local fan.

Tom and Rose had a kindly welcome for all, with a cup of tea and some home-made scones for countless callers over the years. The four McBride children, along with the grand-children, all have memories, more precious than gold, of a home full of love, welcome, music and sport – just a fun place to grow up in.

The McBride household was one of the most welcoming homes you could ever visit. This was often spoken about by many of Tom's fans who became firm friends over the years.

A group of fans from Galway and Mayo visiting Big Tom and Rose at their home in 2016. Left to right: Paddy Naughton, Rusheens, Corofin, John Fallon, Hollymount, County Mayo, Tom Naughton, Bodane, Tuam, Rose McBride, Big Tom McBride, Jarlath Byrne, Corrandulla, and Eamon Byrne, Ballindooley, County Galway.

Media people also experienced the unbridled country hospitality of the McBrides, including some of my own friends and press colleagues.

One media man who has more golden memories of the McBrides than most is their friend, and writer of some of Tom's biggest hits, the well-known journalist and broadcaster Michael Commins.

Michael paid a lengthy and heartfelt tribute to Tom on Midwest Radio on the day that the singer died.

'I was always a fan from National School days. Then in 1975, when Big Tom and The Travellers played their first date in Athy, County Kildare, I was there, and became great friends with Tom and the lads from then on. I wrote the song "Travel On" for their album of the same title, and it was just a change of words from an old American country song,' says Michael.

Other songs written by Michael and recorded by Big Tom include 'The Girl With The Lovely Brown Eyes', 'Tubbercurry My Old Friend' and 'My Old Home In Mayo', to name but a few. He also wrote a number one hit for Susan McCann titled 'Big Tom Is Still The King'.

When Michael left his job as a bank official in County Laois, to follow a career in journalism, he moved first to live in Castleblayney for eight months and became editor of the *Entertainment News* magazine. It was published by Tony Loughman's Top Rank Entertainments agency, which also managed Big Tom at that time. Thus began a lifelong friendship with the McBrides.

'I was visiting at their house a lot during those times, and would often go fishing with Tom to the lakes in South Armagh, even though I knew very little about fishing. That was the time of the Troubles in Northern Ireland, and I used to be absolutely terrified going across those border fields to the lake with Tom,' said Michael in an interview with Gerry Glennon of Midwest Radio.

'A great friendship developed between us, and he was such a modest man, who took success in his stride. There will never be another star like Big Tom. The sadness in the whole country is palpable since he passed away,' added Michael in a voice charged with emotion in that interview.

'Tom had a presence about him when he entered a room, and he had a modesty about him that is so lacking in a lot of humanity nowadays,' he said.

Michael has often quoted something that Rose McBride said to him one evening in Bundoran, seven or eight years ago. This was as the crowds were lining up to dance to Big Tom, hours before he was due on stage.

'The crowds were queuing up outside the hotel, at six or seven on a sunny Sunday evening in June or July. Rose said that Tom turned to her and said that he "couldn't believe that those people were still queuing up" to see him, "after almost fifty years". Rose added, "Isn't it great to have it and not know that you have it?" Her words summed up everything about Big Tom, because some of those stars who think they "have it" can lose it very fast,' added Michael.

Michael is very critical of the snobbery and the cynicism with which many people, in the national media in particular, had viewed Big Tom and his music for decades. But he said it was 'interesting to see' how that had all changed in recent years.

'That snobbery towards Big Tom and Irish country music was ingrained in certain strands of society for years. It took a lot to turn that attitude around, but I'm so glad that it did happen. I will say, in fairness to "The Late Late Show" on RTÉ in more recent times, and indeed to RTÉ in general in more recent times, they changed their tune, but for years they didn't want to know.

'In recent years, there has been a whole new appreciation for that lovely quality which is the rural-ness of Ireland, and an appreciation for the outreach that Tom had with the Irish in England. When Tom went on a stage, he had that ability to get through to everybody in the hall. Not too many singers have that ability, but Margo had it as well,' said the Mayo media and music man. Margo recorded 'The Great Big Tom McBride', which was also penned by Michael.

Michael had Tom booked as the headline artist for his annual country weekend in the Salthill Hotel, Galway, in November 2017. This turned out to be Big Tom's last ever public concert.

So great was the adulation for Tom that night that, as he left the stage, a human avalanche of fans moved swiftly to the side door to shake Big Tom's hands. They completely jammed up the double doorway leading to the side of the stage, to such an extent that American singer Ron Williams was unable to get through the crowd to perform.

The backing band had to strike up and sing 'Galway Bay' to give the Nashville singer sufficient time to get to the stage. On doing so he quipped that, 'Your Big Tom sure is a big star over here.'

On what turned out to be the final night that Tom was ever to perform, Rose was, as usual, there by his side. Sadly, events were to change dramatically for them both, from the sheer joy, exhilaration and excitement of the fans, so palpable at the sold-out concert that night, to the melancholy of the following months.

The death of Rose McBride, who always seemed to be in good health, and who was only seventy-four at the time of her passing, came as a great shock to many. Rose was a very special person, according to Michael Commins. 'Rose was the one that I would almost always ring in the house, and I had such a great friendship with her over the years – she was such a beautiful person and, like Tom, she had no notions about her status in life.

'They were such good-hearted country people that you never had to go to the front door of their home. You could drive in around the yard to the back door, and you could go in without even knocking. The tea would be ready, and sometimes there would be something stronger as well,' said Michael in that radio interview.

He added that the last time he visited Rose was only a few weeks before she passed away, and the welcome was as warm as ever, in fact even warmer!

'It was a cold, wintry Thursday, between Christmas Day and the New Year, and Rose made one of the finest hot whiskeys that I ever had in my life.

'I said to Rose that whatever way she had made that hot whiskey, she should market it, because it could sell around the world, just like Irish coffee does,' he said with a laugh.

He also pointed out that Rose, much like Tom, was highly respected for all the voluntary work that she did in her community, especially for Rehab.

Michael Commins also broadcast the last radio interview of his life-long friend, a few weeks after Rose had passed away. In that live phone-in to Tom's family home, the singer, in a sad and shaky, but still very audible voice, thanked all who had sympathised with the family following the death of Rose.

'It was only about two weeks before he died, and it was his daughter Siobhán that rang me and said that her daddy, as she always called him, had said that he would like to go on my radio show. He wanted to thank everybody for the huge volume of Mass cards and letters of sympathy after Rose's death, and he did that in his own inimitable style,' said Michael, with emotion in his voice.

Above: Rose and Tom among the roses in their garden, with the little hills of Monaghan in the background.
Right: Big Tom receives the Irish Country Entertainer of the Year Award, 1991.

Above: At Ashford Castle in 2016, with daughter Siobhán and grandson Glen. Below: Three cakes, to celebrate (from left) Tom and Rose's twenty-fifth, fortieth and fiftieth wedding anniversaries.

Above: A drummer's-eye view of Big Tom in action.

Below: On board a Ferguson 35 tractor, with a hanger-on.

Above left: Big Tom with the guitar-shaped cake presented by fans to mark the fiftieth anniversary of his first television appearance.

Above right: Sharing a smile with another giant of Irish country, Daniel O'Donnell, at Opry Dhoire, 2017.

Left: Big Tom presents an engraved mirror to the author of this book for his services to country music. On the right is journalist, broadcaster, TV presenter and songwriter Michael Commins, at his annual weekend of concerts in the Salthill Hotel, Galway, 2010.

Above: Pulling pints in The Old Log Cabin.

Right: Madge and her brother Tom at the plaque in Oram, 5 July 2010.

Below: Rose and Tom McBride with their beloved children (from left to right) Thomas, Aisling, Siobhan and Dermot.

Above: The King in the castle – Rose and Big Tom in Ashford Castle in 2016.
Below: Tom with the ones he loved best. Left to right: Dermot and Rita, Austin and Siobhan, Tom and Rose, Aisling, Thomas, Sean Duffy (Aisling's husband) and Rita (Thomas' wife).

Above: Dermot McBride looks up at the clay mould for the statue of his father, in the studio of sculptor Mark Richards in Stanton Lacy, Gloucestershire, United Kingdom. The statue is to be unveiled in Castleblayney town centre in autumn 2018.

Below: The streets of Castleblayney are lined with mourners as Big Tom makes his final journey through the town.

The mural in Oram GAA club dedicated to Big Tom, the King of Irish Country.

Many of the fans became close friends of Big Tom and Rose, and would visit them in their home in Oram. One such fan, who became not just a friend but a volunteer bodyguard for Tom, is Michael O'Donoghue, from Newcastle West, County Limerick.

'It was Rose that first asked me if I would be willing to help him when going on stage, and when getting back down off stage when the show was over.

'I suppose you could call me a fan who became a type of bodyguard for him,' said Michael with a laugh. But while he has been helping Tom on and off the stage for the past two decades or so, the Limerick man knows him a lot longer than that.

'I met him first about forty-five years ago at a dance hall, in The Galtymore ballroom in London, when I was only eighteen. Later on, my wife and I went on our first date to a Big Tom dance, and as the old saying goes, the rest is history.

Big Tom pictured with his voluntary bodyguard Michael O'Donoghue (right) and Michael's wife Helen.

'Ever since, we had a friendship that just grew and grew, so much so that down through the years, when he would be playing in Kerry, he would stay with my wife and myself in our home at The Old Mill in Newcastle West,' said Mike.

He added that the following morning, Tom and Rose, or one of their sons who might be driving them, would travel on to Killarney or wherever he was playing.

Mike and his wife Helen would travel on later that evening to the gig, and they would meet up with Tom afterwards.

'I considered myself a bodyguard for Tom, particularly when he was getting off the stage, because there would be hundreds there coming up to him, praising him, seeking autographs and clapping him on the back.

'Now, if enough people clap you on the back, you will feel it after a while! Tom would come off the stage after two hard hours' performing. But after going to the dressing room to change his clothes and sometimes, only sometimes, grab a quick cup of tea, he would come out and meet the fans, until the last person had left the hall.'

Michael added that when Tom played in the Landmark Hotel, Carrick-on-Shannon, County Leitrim, on 21 June 2016, it was the fiftieth anniversary of Big Tom and The Mainliners performing 'Gentle Mother' on RTÉ's 'The Showband Show'. A group of fans presented him with a guitar-shaped cake to mark the occasion.

'As usual, Tom was gobsmacked that we remembered the anniversary,' said Michael.

Many years ago, in an interview with the *Sunday World*, Rose McBride said she had no problems with girls presenting birthday cake, or standing around the stage after dances looking for her husband's autograph.

'I see lots of girls milling around the stage, and I think it would be a lot worse if they weren't there. Sometimes I get a bit jealous – we are all human.

'Some people say, how can you put up with Tom being away from home working every night of the week. But it's Tom's job, and I accept that,' she said. Tom's fans and friends in many cases became Rose's friends too. She, like her husband, had time for them all, be it visiting their home or talking to them after a gig.

Tom's daughter, Aisling, expressed similar sentiments regarding her famous father's accessibility to all his fans, in an interview with *RSVP* magazine in June 2018. 'He wasn't a big talker, but he was a great listener. He had the same time for everyone,' she said.

Big Tom's voluntary bodyguard Michael O'Donoghue and his wife Helen went to visit him in his home in Oram on Easter weekend 2018, shortly before his health deteriorated.

'He told us that he hoped to go back on stage again and do a few more concerts. Tom seemed determined to go back on stage. However, life didn't give him that chance. But we could also see on that day how heartbroken he was following the death of Rose,' said Michael.

In the interview with *RSVP*, Tom's daughter Aisling also talked about how her parents were a tight-knit team.

'They were a double act, and I think he found it incredibly difficult to be without her. Daddy had always been in and out of hospital, but he was the type to bounce back.

'This time, I think he didn't have the will to fight, he was just broken-hearted. At least they are together now and hopefully out of their suffering,' said Aisling.

In the same interview with *RSVP* magazine, she said that fame never changed her dad.

'You could visit our house and see Daddy in the worse pair of jeans you could find,' she laughed. 'He'd be on an aul tractor in the fields or going up and down the road in a quad. He was unaffected by it all,' she said.

When a reporter and photographer from the *Sunday World* travelled with Big Tom and The Mainliners for a weekend in the early 1970s, they found the late nights tough going.

'It was 4am before Tom and the lads got back to Castleblayney. But Mrs Big Tom met us at the door of their new bungalow just outside the town and we were shown into a sitting room full of trophies, awards and pictures of Tom and the band.

'Big Tom himself joined us shortly afterwards. He said that if he went to bed he wouldn't be able to sleep anyway as the British Army were cratering border roads that morning,' stated the report. Sleep or no sleep, there was welcome for the reporter and photographer in the McBride home, as there always was for everyone.

In a story from a few years later, this time in *New Spotlight* magazine, reporter Julie Boyd wrote about travelling back to Castleblayney with Tom, and members of his new band The Travellers, again in the early hours of a Sunday morning.

'At 7am, 'Blayney was in sight, Harry [Conlon] was first to alight from Tom's Peugeot car, then Kevin [McCooey].

'Big Tom's house was last in line, and on arrival Tom invited us in for a cup of cha,' stated Julie. Once again, as always, a welcome awaited visitors at the McBride family home.

PJ Granaghan, from near Ballina in North Mayo, is another of the many fans who became a family friend of Big Tom and Rose, and he often stayed in their home.

'I would have visited with them for many years, going back to 1971, when I was up in the Castleblayney area. I travelled with Tom to the Rose of Tralee festival that year.

'I often stayed in their home on a Saturday night, but if there was a football match Monaghan were playing in, the dinner would be early on Sunday. He wouldn't want to miss many matches in Clones.'

Those visits by PJ to the McBride home continued up to shortly after Rose passed away.

'I visited him at home only three weeks before he passed away. I thought that his health had improved a bit that evening.

'But the one remark that he made to me when I was leaving will always stick in my mind. Tom shook my hand and said, "Things never will be the same again," and naturally enough he was talking about Rose,' said PJ.

Another visitor to the McBride family home, a fan who also became personal friends with Tom and Rose, as well as supplying them with all their cars for over forty years, is garage owner Gerard Sherlock from Gurteen, County Sligo.

'It was unbelievable really the welcome that always awaited visitors to the McBride home. It was one of the few houses where you just drove into the yard, walked in the back door and the kettle was on immediately.

'That's the kind of relationship that we had with them, and we visited the house so many times. Rose was such a lovely, welcoming woman. I was saddened when I learned that she was ill, and then passed away,' said Gerard.

'One Sunday, shortly before Tom passed away, I visited him in his home and we had a great chat.

'Understandably, he was sad at the loss of Rose. But we sat down around the TV with some of his grandchildren, and watched a Western on the Sky channel.

'He talked about lots of things from the past, and even though he was sad, he was still in good enough form. So it was a shock when Margo [O'Donnell] called me to say he had passed away,' recalled Gerard.

The family friendship between the McBrides and the Sherlocks went much deeper than just a commercial relationship regarding the supply of cars. It was Gerard's brother Father Vincent, who drove from Mayo to celebrate the Month's Mind Mass for Tom in Oram.

Writing in the Mayo News of 22 May 2018, Michael Commins mentioned that Father Vincent Sherlock celebrated Mass earlier that day in Kilkelly, County Mayo, and also 'presided at the First Holy Communion Mass in nearby Kilmovee before heading to County Monaghan for Tom's 4.30 Mass'.

Father Sherlock's brother Gerard said that the two families had become very friendly over the years. 'We had tremendous respect for the McBrides, and I suppose they had similar respect for us.

'When Margo sang "In A Land Where We Never Grow Old" at the Mass, it brought me back to my own father's funeral, which Tom and Rose attended, in Templeronan Cemetery near Gurteen. Tom sang that same song there, and I never will forget it,' added Gerard.

Singer Margo O'Donnell, who moved to live in Castleblayney twenty-five years ago, became one of the closest friends of Rose and Tom McBride, and she visited them regularly.

'We became very close friends, and to be honest, I became part of their family. If I wanted advice I would go to them, and their girls and boys have been wonderful friends too.'

'It seems that I always knew Tom, and since Rose started to travel more with him recently, we met more often, as well as at their home. Her brother Paddy was also in my band for a time,' says Margo.

She says that she was always 'very aware' that not a lot of television coverage was given to Tom over the years.

'Rose and I would sit in their kitchen and speak about this. Then, when the proposal for a "Nationwide" TV special on Tom came up, Rose said it was very important that all the family be part of it. She wanted that more than anything.'

While Margo was a frequent visitor to Rose and Tom's home, she says that very often they would be talking about 'everything and anything', and not always about music.

But when Margo proposed that the local council should erect a statue of Tom in Castleblayney, she says that Rose thought that it would never happen.

Then one day, Margo had an extra spring in her step as she got out of her car and entered the McBride family home.

'I said to Rose, "Guess what?" Rose replied, "What?" It was then I told her that the statue is going ahead.

'Sadly, she knew, and she told me many times, that she wouldn't be here to see it unveiled. Rose seemed to feel that Tom would be around for a while after her, and one night she asked me to write down a few things. She said that when the statue was unveiled, the girls were to stand on one side of Tom and the boys on the other, with the grandchildren all around them,' said Margo, who says she gave that note to the family.

While famous stars such as Margo were among the frequent visitors to Big Tom's home, so also were many of his fans who became firm friends over the years.

One of these is John Pepper. He has spoken elsewhere in this book about how he grew from boy to man listening to the songs of his fellow county man Big Tom.

'Tom was a most obliging man. After a dance in the Horizon Ballroom in Mullingar in April 1978, while chatting to him, I mentioned my curiosity about his recording studio in Castleblayney.

'Tom told me that I'd usually find him in the Old Log Cabin on Monday nights, and invited me to call there and he'd bring me up to the studio. A number of weeks later, I travelled up to Castleblayney late on a Monday evening, and there was Tom and his wife Rose in the Old Log Cabin, in company.'

John added that Tom immediately insisted on buying him a drink. Then, after a short time, he left the company and they headed up to the recording studio.

'Unfortunately – but in hindsight fortunately – when we arrived, it dawned on Tom that he'd left the keys of the studio behind him in the pub. They were with his car keys, as he had travelled in my car.

'While he wanted to get the keys when we arrived back at the Log Cabin, and return to show me around the studio, I insisted on not taking up any more of Tom's personal time. However, that personal time was spent sitting in my car, chatting away outside his pub. Here was a man, although famous, and spoken about in legendary terms, sitting in my car along the street in 'Blayney, chatting away, to someone he didn't know very well at the time,' says John.

John continued that from that evening onwards, he became more acquainted with Tom. 'Sometimes this was much to the frustration of my companion, later my wife, Catherine! I'd have a chat with him after the dances, and get yet another autograph.'

On one such occasion, he mentioned to Tom that he'd like his son, John, to meet him. Without a second thought, Tom said to 'bring him up to the house sometime'. Some weeks later, they arrived in Oram unannounced.

'On the particular evening, Tom and The Travellers were at his house, getting ready to leave for a gig up in Cookstown, County Tyrone.

'He brought us into the house, and to the sitting room where all his awards were. Tom showed us around, without any awareness of time passing. He took time to have my son sit beside him at the piano, while he took John through some of the keys.'

After several photographs were taken with John, Tom presented him with a lovely memento, to mark their visit.

'During all our time with Tom that evening, he gave his complete attention to my son, who was only three years old at the time, without the slightest hint of self-importance.

'This was no different from the story relayed to me by a customer who called into the shop in Oram on a Christmas morning to find Tom, sitting on a bag of potatoes, strumming away on a small guitar with a young boy who'd just received this musical instrument from Santa,' added John.

His mother was also a fan of Tom's first hit, 'Gentle Mother', as well as 'Please Mammy Please', 'The Old Account' and 'The GNR Steam Train'.

In August 1989, the month after Tom and The Mainliners re-formed, John took her, son John and his sister, Bridie, to see them play in Oldcastle, County Meath.

In August 1994, John and his mother called to visit Tom in Oram, bringing John's sons John Junior and Kevin along. That occasion held a very special memory for his mother.

'In the most hospitable, warm and gracious manner, Tom took the time to chat to her, and very comfortably engaged in reminiscing about the era of "The GNR Steam Train" and times gone past.

'He gave my mother a cigarette, and as they lit up, Tom remarked that if we waited for a while, his wife Rose would be back from the cleaners in 'Blayney with his suit for that night's performance, and she'd make tea for us. We declined – I knew my mother was perfectly satisfied to have gotten the cigarette from Big Tom,' concluded John with a laugh.

Another visitor to the McBride home from time to time, a man who straddled the two disciplines of religion and media, was Father Brian D'Arcy, who is well known as the showband priest.

Big Tom said that he always had great respect for Father Brian, since the first time he interviewed him, in the formative days of his music career.

'The first interview that I ever did was with Father Brian D'Arcy, and that was around 1966, or else early '67. I've been great friends with Father Brian since I started out. A lovely man, and he's been a great priest for the showbands. He has a night once a year, either in Edge-worthstown or else in Enniskillen, for all those in the music industry, and it's a great event,' said Tom in an interview for Border Regions TV in 2015.

Big Tom was a shy man, and for a long time in the early part of his career, the interviews that he did were few and far between. At that time, the numbers of fans visiting his home in Oram were fewer too.

This very first interview was conducted under a shroud of secrecy, on a visit to a Catholic monastery in Sligo. This was at the behest of a young clerical student, later destined to become a famous, and sometimes contro-versial, priest, broadcaster and writer – Father Brian D'Arcy.

'I first interviewed Tom for the *Dancing Gazette* magazine, at a time when I wasn't really doing interviews, in 1967. It was in the monastery at Cloonnamahon, near Colooney, County Sligo. It was at a time when, as a student priest, I should have not been even reading papers, let alone writing in them,' says Father Brian.

'I wrote under the pseudonym "Hughie" at that time. I had to smuggle Tom and his manager John McCormick into my room at the top of the monastery to do the interview. Big Tom and the band were playing somewhere nearby that night, and he came and did the interview with me.

'But the word got out later that he had visited the Sligo monastery, and honest to God, there were people shaking hands with me just because I had shook hands with Big Tom. He was a massive star, and because he visited somebody in the monastery, it was a huge thing in the minds of many,' adds Father Brian.

'We laughed about it years afterwards, because Tom had a hard time getting in first with his answers to my questions. His manager John McCormick was very protective of him at the time.

'For example, when I asked Tom what was his next single going to be, before he could answer John McCormick got the answer in first. All Tom could do was nod and smile,' recalls the man known as the showbiz priest.

But as the years went by, and as Father Brian became well known both as a priest and as a broadcaster, his friendship with both Tom and manager John McCormick grew and grew.

Then, about twenty years ago, Father Brian recalls that he did a series of radio programmes for BBC and RTÉ on the showbands. Even then, Tom still wasn't giving many audio interviews. However, he agreed to do one for Father Brian.

'Recently I played it again on BBC Radio Ulster, and it still sounded great, as Tom talked at ease about how he remembered the first day ever that he played a musical instrument.

'He said it was one day when he was only a child and was home from school and in his bed due to illness. He had a mouth organ, and there he was in his bed learning to play a tune on the mouth organ, which he believed was the first full tune that he ever played. Of course, that was long before the fans started visiting his home,' roared Father Brian.

Father Brian relates some other, hitherto untold, stories that he heard from Big Tom, in the next chapter of this book – some of them also about things that happened long before the fans started to come visiting the home of their idol in Oram.

Visiting Big Tom and Rose in the kingdom they called home became almost a ritual for many fans and friends of the McBrides over the years. In the same spirit as the lines in the Richard Thompson song, recorded by Sean Keane, 'From Galway to Graceland to be with the King', about a fan going to the grave of Elvis, Margo says there will always be people visiting the McBrides' grave in Oram churchyard.

'Rose and Tom always loved people calling to their home, and since they have passed away, I have seen people now coming to their grave in the local churchyard.

'Very often, when I call to the grave to say prayers for them both, other people are there also, paying their respects. Before I walk away I silently think, "The people are still visiting,"' said Margo with a tear in her eye.

Chapter 10

Stars Remember Tom and He Remembers Them

Big Tom said he was delighted that younger stars, such as Daniel O'Donnell and Nathan Carter, were doing so much television work. But he wasn't that fond of being on the small screen himself. He told me, roaring with laughter, that he always felt there would be 'too many looking at us on TV'.

However, an eclectic assortment of personalities, from rock and country musicians to religious and political figures, have graciously showed their respect and admiration for Tom when recalling their memories of him.

Such stars range from rockers like Shane McGowan, who invited Tom to his birthday party only weeks before Tom passed away, to The Edge from U2, Una Healy of The Saturdays, Johnny Gallagher of trad-rock band Boxty, and Tom's old and younger buddies on the country scene.

Big Tom was, to quote the title of a Merle Haggard album, a 'Poet of the Common Man'. He was all that, and more, to his fans, and to many other singing and performing stars who became his friends. Big Tom was also loved for his warm-hearted ways. Quiet and unassuming, he always had a quick wit. He was good company, he was good humoured and he was never one for caustic comments or derogatory remarks about others.

Perhaps it was the sincerity in his voice, or maybe the sincere sentimentality in many of his songs, that touched the hearts and minds of so many fans in a way that no other Irish country singer could. Big Tom sounded distinctively different to the rest.

Country 'n' Irish Queen Margo O'Donnell is one of a number of Irish country stars who sound distinctively different too. No fake American country twang for her either. While it might seem a tenuous comparison, one could, in a far-fetched way, liken them

Friends and neighbours Big Tom and Margo O'Donnell.

both to the distinctive design of a Coca-Cola contoured glass bottle: The man who designed it wanted it to be so distinctive that, even in the dark, when you held the bottle you instantly knew it was Coke. Close your eyes and listen to any song by Big Tom or Margo, and, if you are a fan of Irish country music, you will instantly recognise the distinctive voice of either of those two singers.

The Donegal country songstress was also the last to record a duet hit with Tom, and this will always be an abiding memory for her.

'Neither of us was touring at the time, and we recorded it for personal reasons. It was as friends, and not as artists, we recorded it. But I have to say, that record has been the pinnacle of my recording career,' said Margo.

Margo recalled that when she found the song that she thought might be suitable, written by Donegal's Shunie Crampsey, she took it out to the McBrides' home, for Tom to have a listen. He was, Margo said, 'very slow to say anything'.

'I played it a second time, and after that he said, "Put it on again there," and when it was finished I said, "Well, what do you think?" In his usual unhurried fashion, Tom replied, "It's a nice wee song alright." Then I was so delighted when he asked, "Will we record it?"' said Margo.

Meanwhile, in an interview published in the summer of 2017 in Daniel O'Donnell's International Fan Club magazine, Tom told me that he and Rose had many memories of Margo from her early days as a singing star, as well as of her brother Daniel.

One could say that Daniel's recording career had a royal birth, as his first single, 'My Donegal Shore', was recorded at the studio of the King, Big Tom's Studio, Castleblayney.

Tom said that, while he wasn't present for that recording session, he remembered Daniel from much earlier times. The McBrides' and the

O'Donnells' friendship goes back to when Daniel's mother Julia, and his sister Margo, would often visit Rose and himself in Oram.

'I remember Daniel as a young lad, sometimes calling here with his mother and Margo. They would be travelling the long journey from Donegal to Dublin, when Margo would be playing at a dance or concert there.

'There was always a cup of tea for them here at our house, and we might even have a bit of a sing-song before they went on their way. It was a long trip to Dublin from Donegal for Margo, who was only a young girl at that time. So it was nice for them to be able to break the journey here along the way.

'Of course, Margo and myself sometimes met when we toured in the Irish dancehalls in England. But because we might be both touring at the same time in different parts of the country, our paths did not cross that regularly.

'However, we would meet from time to time, especially if both bands were in London on the same weekend. Later on, I remember Daniel as a young man, coming to many of our dances in Dublin and elsewhere, sometimes when we also played in London,' said Tom.

While Tom says it is hard to predict where any young singer will go in the music business, he always liked the way Daniel conducted himself in those early days:

'He always has a way with him; he was a nice, personable young man with a good voice, and there was no messing about him – he always called a spade a spade, and whatever he planned to do he was upfront in telling you.'

When Daniel started recording, it was with 'My Donegal Shore', written by the late Johnny McCauley. At the time, the Irish-born but London-based songwriter was penning most of Big Tom's hits.

'I think it may have been some months after I recorded "My Donegal Shore" in Nashville for the *Blue Wings* album that Daniel recorded the song in my studio in Castleblayney. I was not around when he did the recording, but I was very impressed when I heard his version later.

'It was a song that did a lot for me, as well as for Daniel. Johnny had a great gift for writing songs. I know that Daniel recorded others that he has written, including "The Pretty Little Girl From Omagh", also recorded by Larry Cunningham, and "Any Tipperary Town". Johnny had this happy knack of putting stories into songs that meant a lot to the people listening. Once he got an idea for a song, or even if you gave him enough details about a subject, he could create a song very quickly,' he added.

Big Tom said that he was delighted and amazed at all the places around the world that Daniel O'Donnell plays in – but he would never fly that far and certainly never that often.

'Daniel is a big star in places that I would never even visit. As I said, I am not fond of flying. While I went to America, it was the boat for me mostly when going abroad, usually for regular trips to play in England.

'Daniel obviously has no fear of flying, and he has become popular in so many countries that so very few Irish artists ever went to. He seems to get on well wherever he goes.'

Big Tom says that while he had never been too keen on television appearances either, he enjoyed being on a few programmes with Daniel, especially 'in the last couple of years'.

'Daniel is very comfortable on TV, but it is something that I was never comfortable with. I always felt that there are too many looking at you when you are on TV.'

'But I enjoyed being on the Irish Country Music Awards show on RTÉ, which was presented very professionally, and with ease, by Daniel. We were both on the "Late Late Show" Country Specials a few times with Ryan Tubridy, which were enjoyable too,' he added.

Tom also felt at ease when Daniel presented a television special about his life, during which they both sang songs made popular by Tom for the 'Opry Dhoire' series. It was shown on TG4 in Ireland, and also on BBC Alba, the Scottish Gaelic channel, during 2017.

Tom also said that Daniel 'was very brave' to go on 'Strictly Come Dancing', as 'that had to be nerve-wracking' for anyone to do.

'He had a hell of a lot of nerve to go on that programme. He was going on a top British TV show, alongside people who had spent years learning dancing and doing dances of different styles.

Tom and Daniel with their handprints in bronze, on the day that they were given the Freedom of Cong.

'But Daniel seemed to fit into that show without a bother, and even if he didn't win, he was very good the nights that he was on. Everybody had so much respect for him, because he was willing to give it a go.'

Tom said that even though he and Daniel met from time to time, mostly backstage at concerts or before and after television shows, they never got around to talking about songs that they had both recorded.

'There never seemed to be enough time to talk about the same songs that we did. But he is so very busy anyway, and we never had time for long conversations during those casual meetings. Daniel's career is flying high all over the world, and it couldn't happen to a nicer fellow.'

In common with Daniel, wherever Big Tom played, the venues were always packed. He praised the air plays on local radio, and the videos being broadcast on various television channels in recent years, for having a big bearing on the increased popularity of country music, especially in Ireland and England.

'One time, when you recorded a song, you would be lucky to get a play or two for it on radio, and TV appearances were very few indeed.

'But it all changed in recent years and became much easier to get air plays since so many local radios became successful in Ireland. Seemingly, it is less bother to get on TV shows too,' added Tom.

'Some singers have their own TV shows now, but it is something that I would not be into – I wouldn't want too much television,' smiled Tom, who once turned down the opportunity to do his own series on RTÉ. That was because he couldn't have The Mainliners backing him, and would have had to work with session musicians.

'They were great musicians at what they did. But some of them did not have the feel for country music,' said Tom when walking away from doing his own television series in the early 1970s.

During the interview, published in Daniel's magazine in March 2017, it was mentioned to Big Tom that a DVD and CD titled *A Celebration* had some shots of him on television, singing some of his best-known songs. His answer was a slightly humorous one:

'Sure, we had to let the people know that I am still here and still doing a bit! Bringing out new releases and playing for dancers is what I have been doing for most of my life.

'Thankfully, most of the records that we released over the years usually worked well for us,' he added.

When asked during that interview what the secret of his longevity on the music scene was, Tom's reply could well have been paraphrased from the words of the Frank Sinatra song 'I Did It My Way'.

'Well, I suppose it was because we did songs our way, and we didn't try to copy anyone else's style. As a dance band, we had a different sound to a lot of the other bands. Just like Daniel, I've had a great life in the music business,' he said.

At the conclusion of that interview, Big Tom said that 'there had been talk' about him doing a duet with Margo O'Donnell. Of course that record came out since, and was a hit, but sadly, it was to be the last single featuring the voice of the King of Irish Country.

But, as Margo points out, Tom has left behind a great legacy of music. Margo was the first person that I heard refer to him as 'Ireland's Johnny Cash', on the first 'Late Late Show' Country Special a few years ago. Nathan Carter also paid him the same compliment on the 'Late Late Show' tribute to Tom.

Another star who duetted with Margo, during the earlier days of their careers, was the late Larry Cunningham. He was also a contemporary of

Big Tom. With their two bands, Tom and Larry were the biggest stars among Irish emigrants in the UK in the 1960s and 1970s. In a tribute programme on the late Larry Cunningham on TG4's 'Opry Dhoire' series last autumn, Tom recalled Larry and said why the Longford singer was such a success.

'Larry was a real down-to-earth country singer. You can't make them; they are born,' he said.

Daniel O'Donnell says that the first time he saw Big Tom perform was when he was a teenager, attending a recording of his sister Margo's television show. Daniel added that the first striking feature about Tom was how big he looked.

'This is a young person's memory of him, and I think that he was sitting on a stool, singing and strumming a guitar. I just thought how big in stature he was.

'We knew his music very well in our house, since the days of "Gentle Mother" when I was only a child. Then going forward, I can remember all the other hits he had, but in particular when "Four Country Roads" was such a big hit,' said the Donegal crooner.

Daniel explains about an image that is still somewhere in the 'caverns of his mind', to borrow one of the lines from that Big Tom hit, about exactly where he was when he first heard it on radio.

'I remember it being played on a radio programme that came out over the sound system on a bus that I was travelling on from Donegal to Dublin. I have this distinct memory of hearing it just as we were about to step off in Monaghan for the tea break during the bus journey,' he added.

'I used to go dancing to Big Tom and The Travellers in the Ierne Ballroom when I was working in Dublin, and I always felt what a big star he was.

But he was always so humble about his success, and that was something that he held on to right to the very end.

'We did the "Opry Dhoire" show with him for TG4 in late 2017, and no doubt about it, I felt that I was in the presence of greatness. It's not something that's easy to quantify – it's immeasurable and indescribable. But when you are in the presence of someone that has that natural gravitas, you realise it,' added Daniel.

'It was such a shock to hear he had passed away, as we sometimes think people like him will go on forever. I think Rose's death had a huge impact on Tom, as she was so supportive of him. In recent times, Rose was only a step away from him all the time.

'In the early days, when she was raising the children, not many people saw Rose. It was only in later years that I saw a lot more of Rose, at concerts and TV shows such as "Opry Dhoire" or "The Late Late Show". She was always there for him over the decades, but in particular, when Tom's health wasn't as good during the latter years,' said Daniel.

He added that Rose was extremely proud of all that Tom had achieved during his career.

'One of the nicest things she said was that "it was great to see how people loved what he did", and that they saw him as a star. But Tom was the last person to think of himself as a star. He never thought about that or dwelt upon it either,' added Daniel.

That recording of 'Opry Dhoire' with Daniel for TG4 in the autumn of 2017 was to be Big Tom's last full live concert. But he did a guest appearance on a fundraising concert in Donegal with Daniel, Nathan Carter and others shortly afterwards, as Daniel recalls.

'We were doing a fundraising show in Letterkenny for the Donegal flood victims, and Tom got in touch with me, saying, "You know, the Donegal people were good to me down through the years, and I'd like to take part in that fundraiser," and he came and sang four songs.

'As usual, when he got up on the stage, the people just loved him – as they did a few years earlier, when himself and myself sang on a stage on a rainy evening when we were given the "Freedom of Cong" in Mayo. We both had bronze replicas of our hands displayed in the town,' he added.

Daniel says that at this and similar events, 'during the last few years', he got to spend more time talking with Tom than in all the previous years.

'It was great to do stuff with him on stage during the last while, as before that, our paths only rarely crossed in a professional way, because we were both touring in different places.

'However, the Cong event, and the "Opry Dhoire" show, gave me an opportunity to spend more time with him than ever before. He was a very nice, down-to-earth man, who was shy and almost dismissive about all he had achieved, which was a lovely trait in him. Big Tom will be missed, but never forgotten,' concluded Daniel.

* * *

Now, to change the scene to a different time and place – can you, the reader, picture the next moment, frozen in time in the mind of another friend and fan? The scene is of a tall, lanky Longford teenager, knocking sparks off the rough road surface with his leather-soled shoes. He is singing 'Gentle Mother' as he heads towards 'The Old School Yard', at the technical school in Ballinamuck in 1966. That lanky Longford lad was later to become nationally known as singer Mick Flavin.

'I remember learning the words of that song off the sponsored pro-grammes on the radio, and singing it while walking along the road to school. The only radio station we listened to then was Radio Éireann. We had no TV, and were lucky enough to have an auld record player in our house.

'About two years later, after finishing school, I also remember cycling with a few other lads, all friends of mine, as we rode our battered auld bicycles to a marquee in County Leitrim, just to hear Big Tom and The Mainliners play,' added Mick.

Over twenty years later, Mick was playing with his band at The Galtymore in London one Saturday night. Just after finishing their set, who should walk in and over to him but Big Tom. He was also playing in London that weekend, and he wanted to chat with Mick, who was 'delighted and honoured' to have a photo taken with him.

'I also saw him a few times at The Marquee in Drumlish after that, when Declan Nerney had him playing there. Then, when our other singing colleague, Noel Cassidy, died in 2017, Tom came to the church and both of us sang at the funeral.

'Sadly, I was at Tom's funeral less than a year later, but I was honoured to sing a bit of "Wildflowers" at his grave. He was a lovely man, and I think that when Rose died, a major part of Tom died as well,' said Mick.

The biggest song of all, about Big Tom, launched the career of Susan McCann. It was 'Big Tom Is Still The King', which took her from near obscurity to number one, and national stardom, in 1977. The song stayed for almost three months in Ireland's Top Thirty.

The song was written by Michael Commins, who cleverly, and excellently, changed the words of the Waylon Jennings hit in the US 'Bob Willis

Big Tom and Susan McCann on the shores of Lough Muckno, when her song 'Big Tom Is Still The King' was at number one.

Is Still The King'. He gave it an Irish slant about Big Tom that struck a chord with record buyers everywhere.

'My memories are of joining Tony Loughman's Top Rank Entertainments agency, and Tony saying to me that he had a song in the office for months which he thought could be a big hit for me.

'Tony said, "If the Big Tom fans like it, as I think they will, it will get your name out there all over the country." So I recorded it in the studio in Castleblayney that was later to become Big Tom's Studio. We released it as a single, and sure the rest is history,' said Susan.

It went to number one within weeks, much to the annoyance of some music critics, especially in Dublin.

'Many of them looked down their noses at the success of Big Tom at that time. Some of them even said they would build a bonfire in 'Blayney and put themselves on top of it if it made number one.

'Of course, it went all the way to the top of the pop charts, but we didn't see any of those critics on top of a bonfire in 'Blayney,' she roared.

This was at a time when singles had to sell in thousands to even make the charts. The album that was released afterwards, with the song on it, also sold in thousands for Susan, and she was well on her way, not just to national stardom, but to major international success later as well.

'I remember too, long before I started singing professionally, many times when myself and my husband Dennis, who was then my boyfriend, would travel all over Northern Ireland to see Big Tom and the band play.

'I will always hold in my mind memories of Ford's Cross Carnival, and all the other carnivals that he played at. We even went as far as Kingscourt in County Cavan from Newry one Sunday night, which was a long trip for us back then, just to see him play. Other great memories are of nights that he played in The Commercial in Dungannon,' said the singer now known as the First Lady of Irish Country.

'Can you just imagine how excited I was then when I got to record the song about Big Tom? And he became very supportive of me for doing it. We had a photo shoot done of the two of us beside Lough Muckno near Castleblayney, and Big Tom, gentleman that he was, said the song was also good for his career.'

Susan was interviewed on the 'Late Late Show' tribute to Big Tom after he passed away. An iconic photo of her and Tom, taken all those years earlier, was splashed across TV screens, on social media, and on most national and regional newspapers as well.

'I remember Tom wishing me well after that photo taken down by the lake. I can still hear him saying, "Remember, Susan, when recording, always do a song that the postman can whistle or sing – something that everyone can sing along with." He was 100 percent right,' said Susan.

'How could I ever forget how the crowds at my dances just swelled almost overnight after "Big Tom Is Still The King" topped the charts? The Big Tom fans came out to hear me, and stuck with me ever since,' said Susan, who sang a verse of 'Big Tom Is Still The King' at Tom's graveside during his funeral.

Country star Declan Nerney says he can appreciate why his niece, international pop star and founding member of The Saturdays Una Healy, put a photo of herself and Declan and a message on instagram following Tom's death. She was recalling her cherished memories of meeting Big Tom at The Marquee in Drumlish.

'Very sad news this morning. RIP Big Tom. A true legend and inspiration for so many people in Irish country music. Big Tom – King of Country – so lucky to have met him when we performed at The Marquee in Drumlish, pictured here with my uncle Declan in 2016,' stated the international pop star.

'Of course, Una had great respect for Big Tom, as she appreciates where he came from and where I also come from musically. She knew that he was the music well where I got the inspiration from,' said her uncle Declan.

Una Healy had thousands of likes from followers on instagram when she posted that photo of herself with Big Tom and her uncle, on the day that Big Tom died.

Declan Nerney likens Big Tom and The Mainliners to The Beatles or The Rolling Stones, but in the country genre.

'That sound of Big Tom and The Mainliners will never be equalled again. It's a bit like The Beatles or The Rolling Stones, as all these boys grew up together. They were around the same age, and they created something that was never there before, and it will be there for generations to come. It takes a whole new generation of people to come up with something like that,' said Declan.

Those sentiments are echoed somewhat in some lines of a story written by Eileen Casey in *Ireland's Own* magazine on 25 May 2018.

'It all began when, with Henry McMahon, and five other local youths, in the mid-'sixties The Mainliners were formed (originally called The Mighty Mainliners). The group appeared on RTÉ's "Showband Show" with "Gentle Mother" and the rest is C&W history,' stated the story.

So perhaps one could compare the practising and playing in the tin shed or the old school in Oram with a few other boys from Liverpool doing likewise in The Cavern?

Declan Nerney, who made the comparison between The Mainliners and The Beatles, had a hit himself with 'The Marquee In Drumlish', co-written with the bandleader of The Mainliners, Henry McMahon. Henry also penned 'The Ballad Of

A heartfelt social media message from Una Healy upon the death of Big Tom.

Big Tom' for Declan, and the Longford singer presented Tom with a crystal glass replica of the Sam Maguire Cup at The Marquee in Drumlish in 2016, decades after he first saw Big Tom sing.

'I saw him first as a gossoon [youngster] of only twelve, playing in The Marquee in Drumlish in 1968. Forty years later, I brought him back there again. It's incredible to think that Tom and The Mainliners sounded exactly the same as they did forty years earlier.

'There were young people there that night who were at the Oxygen rock festival earlier that day in Kildare. They said there was no act in the Oxygen festival that created the same euphoria as Big Tom and The Mainliners created that night. Don't forget that Big Tom was from their grandparents' generation, yet they were still in awe of him,' said Declan, who also led the backing music for all the singers in a farewell to Big Tom at his burial in Oram.

Two nights previously, when the 'Late Late Show' tribute to Big Tom was recorded, Declan was also on hand, with his lead guitar, to play along with others as many of Ireland's biggest country stars sang Big Tom songs. They all shared their memories of the big man from 'Blayney with the studio audience and the nation.

One of those performers, who sang 'Gentle Mother' to his own acoustic guitar accompaniment, was the biggest young country star to emerge in Ireland in recent years, Nathan Carter.

'I didn't get to talk much to Big Tom when first I met him, after I played support to him when only eighteen, and as a one-man band, at the closing dance in The Galtymore in London. But I got to chat with him when I did a couple of gigs with him since.

'I performed at Roscommon Racecourse on the day that Tom also performed there, a couple of years back.

'Then in 2017, we did a charity gig in Letterkenny, County Donegal, myself and Daniel [O'Donnell] and Big Tom, to help raise money for the flood victims of Inishowen and Derry,' said Nathan, recalling some memories of meeting Big Tom in a story in the *Irish World* newspaper of 29 April 2018.

Nathan added: 'I got to chat with Big Tom that day. He said congratulations on my success, and I replied, "To be honest, all the biggest memories I've got from starting out was that night in the Galty." To this, Tom responded, "It was a memorable one for us all."

'In my live shows I'm doing a medley, a tribute to Big Tom, this year. We're doing it on the shows around Ireland as a way to pay tribute to his songs and his career.

'I don't think there will be anyone else like Big Tom who will come along. There's definitely going to be singers who come and go, and sing country songs, but he was just a total once-off,' said Nathen in that interview.

Another admirer of Tom's is trad-rocker Johnny Gallagher of Boxty, the group that also has his two brothers in it. They play for many Harley-Davidson gigs around the world, and for the royal family in Monaco, according to Father Brian D'Arcy.

'It's amazing how Johnny Gallagher and Big Tom McBride, who came from two polar opposites on the music scene, gelled when they got together for a music session. That was after one of my retreats for the music fraternity at The Graan Monastery in Enniskillen,' said Father Brian in an interview for this book.

'Johnny was doing rock leads and amazing chord things on his guitar, and Tom loved it as he sang "Gentle Mother" along with him. It showed how he loved all music, and respected musicians who were different to him, as Johnny is one of the best rock guitarists in Europe, and Boxty play to thousands in Italy.

'The reason the two fellows gelled was because Tom was respected for his musical ability, his talent and his sincerity by people from so many music genres. That was because Tom was himself, not copying anyone, and he was a roots musician's dream.

'Anybody who was interested in real music knew that Tom was real, and therefore respected his version of his real music. As The Edge from U2 said: "Big Tom was a legend."'

Big Tom was the first person to be inducted into the Irish Country Music Hall of Fame, on RTÉ in 2016. On that occasion, one of those to pay tribute to him was legendary songwriter and frontman of The Pogues, Shane McGowan, famous for such songs as 'Fairytale Of New York', 'The Irish Rover', 'A Pair Of Brown Eyes' and many more.

'He was always on the radio, and they were always playing ya know. It was just good music ya know. Big Tom is still the King,' said Shane.

When interviewed for this book, Tom's daughter Aisling said that there was an email to their home a few weeks before her dad died. It was an invitation from Shane McGowan to attend his sixtieth birthday celebration, which was being held in Monaghan.

'It was such a nice gesture of Shane to email with the invitation, but sadly Daddy was not well enough to attend the party,' said Aisling. She added that the family were 'so delighted' that Shane McGowan thought so much

The social media generation: Big Tom with (from left): Derek Ryan, Mike Denver and Nathan Carter.

of their father. Shane McGowan also included a photo of Big Tom on the inside sleeve of his album *Crock of Gold*, which shows the respect that he has for The King of Irish Country.

So, while Big Tom has crossed the great divide, and gone on to the next world, it's plain to see that many diverse stars, from many music genres, remember and revere him as an iconic figure in Irish showbusiness. Tom's songs have also crossed many music divides, from country to pop and rock, in this world.

Chapter 11

A President Mourns a Monarch

Words from the song 'The Day Elvis Died' by the late, great US country singer Boxcar Willie, described years ago by President (then Deputy) Michael D Higgins on Galway Bay FM as one of his favourite country performers, are thought-provoking.

Perhaps those song words can resurrect, in your mind's eye, where you were at the time when you were first informed that your hero, whoever he or she was, had died.

In the song 'The Day Elvis Died', Boxcar Willie is saying to his son that he understands why he 'cried the day Elvis died'. It seems that he (Boxcar) 'cried all day' himself when his hero Hank 'was called away', back in 1953.

Some of us, of more mature years, remember exactly where we were when we heard that US President John F Kennedy was killed, or when Martin Luther King or Bobby Kennedy were assassinated. Others, of younger years, remember where they were when they heard that Elvis had died.

Fans of Big Tom will remember clearly where they were when they first heard, or read, that their King of Country had passed away. That moment of sudden sadness will forever remain etched in the memories of so many.

To say that Big Tom was a hero to many generations of Irish at home, and abroad, is almost an understatement. One such person, who during his student days was an emigrant in London and is now the holder of the highest office in Ireland, is President Michael D Higgins.

The President, himself a staunch supporter and champion of all forms of music, arts and culture generally, personally paid his respects to Big Tom as the singer's body lay in repose in his beloved Oram.

President Higgins travelled there to convey the sympathy of the country, as well as to pay his own personal respects, to the McBride family. In doing so, he was honouring what the songs of their famous father had meant to Irish people at home and overseas.

He spoke to the family privately, and viewed the trophies and awards that Tom had amassed during his half-a-century as an entertainer, displayed in the McBride's home. The words of President Higgins's public tribute also epitomised what the music of Big Tom had meant to so many:

President Michael D Higgins examines some of the awards and mementoes of a life in country music.

Lovers and supporters of Irish music everywhere will have heard the news of the death of Big Tom McBride with sadness.

As one of the most charismatic and influential artists in Irish country music, Big Tom was widely respected, and through his five decades of music making he leaves a lasting legacy.

His name will be recalled with fond memory by those who listened, and danced to, his and his band members' generous nights of entertainment all over the island of Ireland.

A big personality and one of the country's greatest country stars, his love of music and his passion and skill have enriched Ireland's music scene.

As President of Ireland, I wish to express my deepest sympathies to his children Thomas, Dermot, Aisling and Siobhán, the members of his family, his friends and to the countless numbers of people, at home and abroad, who loved the man and his music.

A monarch paid her respects too – an Irish Queen who knew Tom well.

Country music Queen Philomena Begley spoke about her memories of Tom's great sense of humour, when they would meet backstage, at concerts or prior to television appearances.

'I was on the scene a wee bit before him with the Old Cross Céili Band. I remember him very well from the early days, and I always had great admiration for him down through the years. He had a unique singing style, and I always said that if you couldn't dance to the music of Big Tom, then you just couldn't dance,' said Philomena.

She continued: 'The beat that he had in his music was unreal, and he always picked great songs, songs that he loved to sing. I remember my father saying to me to "always sing songs you enjoy singing", and how true that is.

'Tom was also great company to be with at the concerts and shows that we were on together over the years. He was always so witty with his remarks, and whenever in his company, we always had some great laughs behind the scenes,' added Philomena with a laugh.

'Tom just loved singing, just like I do. There is a great buzz every time you go out on stage,' said the seventy-five-year-old Queen of Country.

She says that in the last year or two, their paths did not cross as much, except for the television shows that they were on together, and at an open-air concert in Roscommon Racecourse. On that occasion, they 'talked backstage for ages'.

Taoiseach Leo Varadkar, who is from a younger generation of Irish people and who one might expect not to be so familiar with Big Tom's music, paid him a wholesome tribute too.

The Taoiseach described Big Tom as 'a giant in Irish country music for over fifty years'.

'With his band The Mainliners, he filled dance halls the length and breadth of the country. His songs were a reflection of Irish life, and an important connection for the Irish diaspora.

'Not many people are known by their first name, but that was Big Tom. It shows his popularity and legendary status as the King of Irish Country Music,' added an Taoiseach.

Fianna Fáil leader Micheál Martin tweeted that he was 'very sad' when he heard the news of Big Tom's death. He said the late singer 'charmed and entertained so many over the years'.

The Minister for Culture, Heritage and the Gaeltacht, Josepha Madigan, said: 'Big Tom made a huge contribution to Irish country music during his career, spanning five decades.

'He and his band The Mainliners were a fixture of dancehalls and ball-rooms in the 'sixties and 'seventies, earning him the title of the King of Irish Country Music,' the Minister continued.

'His songs not only connected with people in Ireland, but also with Irish people abroad, bringing joy to the many Irish diaspora across the globe.'

Concluding in Irish, the Minister added: 'Ní bheidh a leithéid arís ann.'

Sinn Féin's European Parliament member for the Connacht–Ulster con-stituency, Matt Carthy, also issued a statement expressing his sadness at the news of Big Tom's death.

'Big Tom was Monaghan's most loved son, and a great ambassador for the county. In many respects he invented the "Country and Irish" genre. A major figure in Irish country music for over fifty years, Big Tom was hugely popular, not just in Ireland, but among the Irish diaspora, especially among Irish emigrants in Britain.

He added: 'He will be sadly missed by people across all generations, and especially by people from Monaghan, who have always been proud of our association with him,' added the MEP.

While these cultural, political and other society figures, along with the legions of fans, were all saddened at the loss of Big Tom, his passing inevitably tugs hardest at the heartstrings of the family he loved.

'People will miss the entertainer, but we will miss the man. I can't imagine what life will be like without him,' said his daughter Aisling Duffy, in an interview with *RSVP* magazine.

And family was so important to Big Tom and Rose, who were so happy that all of their children and grandchildren lived close by them. Tom said so to me during that interview in his home which has been interspersed throughout this book.

'All our family are living around here – the furthest away would be our daughter Aisling, who lives across the border in Cullyhanna, County Armagh, which is only about five miles away.

'The rest of the family are living so near to us here that you could nearly throw a stone and reach their homes. Dermot was playing with us during the last few years that we were playing, and he will be on the next tour with us. But when I stopped playing three years ago, Dermot stopped playing too,' said Big Tom in that 2004 interview.

With a laugh, he added, 'The young fellow will have to get the guitar shined up and tuned up again for our next tour.'

During that interview, he also spoke about the time when his eldest son, Thomas, was a teenager and also showed an interest, for a while, in going into the music business.

'Thomas had a great interest in music for a while, and he was drumming with a few local bands, and with my band The Travellers for a time.

But he didn't follow it up – I think he might have got tired of the road,' laughed Tom.

Tom had been off the road for three years at the time that he did that interview with me in 2004. He said that it was mainly because of requests from the fans around Ireland that he had decided to go back and do some touring again with The Mainliners.

'We were being contacted by people from all over the place, asking us to go back on tour one more time. Anyway, that's why we are doing so. What had made me stop was that I had got tired of the travelling, and I was also having problems with my voice.

'So I thought it best to take a break away from it all, which was nearly three years ago. But the voice is back in good shape, and as I've no problem singing again, the batteries are recharged and I'm rarin' to go,' roared the gentle giant of country with laughter.

Father Brian D'Arcy, who earlier in this book reminisced about his memories of Tom and Rose McBride and how much they were respected in Oram, and who was a personal friend of the family for fifty years, also described him as a 'lovely, gentle man'.

'He was the one that everybody looked up to. He was the one that probably the elitists sort of looked down their noses at, and Big Tom outlasted them all,' Father D'Arcy said.

'At his last gig, he was able to bring a thousand people into his show, who still adored the ground he walked on; who still loved him as a friend and as a singer; who still appreciated what he had done for them. Who still made their hearts want to dance every time he opened his mouth and sang. Tom was one of themselves, but he was their King as well.'

Father Brian added that Big Tom's outreach to Irish emigrants in the UK during the showband years was unrivalled.

'Big Tom brought Ireland to the Irish emigrants in lonely times. He sang about their life, about their mother, their family, their homeland, their joys and sorrows too.

'Tom was like the poet Patrick Kavanagh, another Monaghan man, and neither of them got the respect they deserved in the beginning,' continued Father Brian. 'Kavanagh was not respected either in the beginning. He was looked upon as an amadán and a fool from the country. There were people, around Dublin in particular, who thought Tom was singing bullshit when he sang songs about mothers, and emigrants longing to come home.

'Eventually people discovered that Tom was the one with the true art, and he was respected for that, just as Kavanagh eventually was. It came a little too late, but nevertheless, at least more so than Patrick Kavanagh, Big Tom lived to experience some of that respect during his own life,' pointed out Father Brian.

'The longer that time went by, the more people discovered that both Tom and Patrick Kavanagh had the art of talking, writing and singing in their own words, and making that language a universal theme.

'I've said it on "The Late Late Show", and I'll say it again and again, there is a kind of a hole in our heart that can't be filled. Also there is a hole in the culture of Ireland that has passed away and can never be replaced,' he added.

Many of those who grew up with Tom have alluded to the fact that if it wasn't for fate, and tragedy, he wouldn't have come back to Ireland. Tom recalled that too, in an interview on another RTÉ show, 'A Little Bit Country', back in 2006.

'At the time I had no plans for settling in Ireland, so if I hadn't got that sad message from home, about my young brother having died, I could still be in Jersey.'

With his usual wit, Big Tom injected a bit of humour into the conversation by adding, 'I could still be laying pipes over there.'

Also on the humorous side, Father Brian remembered a time when Tom told him that when he started out with a céilí band after coming home, they 'used to get gigs in the Congo'.

'I was thinking, "How could Big Tom and the band have gone to the Congo to play gigs?" Then Tom explained to me that this was during his time with the Finncairn Céilí Band, the forerunners to The Mainliners.

'All was explained, as "the Congo" was a name that locals had put on a dancehall down the road from Castleblayney, on the Keady side.

'It was a hall that people went to on a Sunday night, but very often some people went there just to finish fights that began on the football fields earlier that day,' roared Father Brian.

'Nearly every Sunday night, there would be a fight at the dances there, and because the Civil War was raging in the Congo at that time in the early 1960s, the locals used to call this wee hall "the Congo".

'When he mentioned the name to me first, I thought for a moment that Tom had gone off to Africa to play. But instead of that, it was just up the road from Castleblayney,' laughed Father Brian.

He also said that Tom told him that those dances were at a time when the GAA ran dances. There were certain restrictions put on the bands, regarding what they were and weren't allowed to play.

'They weren't allowed to play anything only Irish music for the first part of the dance. Seamus McMahon and the other boys in the band would play all that.

'Then, when the medals were presented to the winning team, the GAA officials would go home and the band could do what was called "céilí" and "old-time music".'

Ireland was changing culturally in the 1960s, and the bands were very much at the coal face of those cultural changes. They had to start making their musical programmes more varied, and to include what were basically old-time waltzes.

'Big Tom was the old-time part of his band, as was Philomena Begley when she started out with the Old Cross Céilí Band.

'They were only singing a couple of country songs a night at first, and then eventually their bands became ones that played country music for most of their live programmes,' he added.

The showbiz priest also said that songwriter Johnny McCauley should always be mentioned 'in the same breath' as Big Tom in any tribute.

'Both Tom and Larry Cunningham always gave great credit to Johnny for the songs that he wrote for them. He penned "Among The Wicklow Hills" and others for Larry, plus so many hits for Tom later on,' said Father Brian.

Young singer Mike Denver spoke about a very different and very laudable characteristic of Big Tom's easy-going manner, which was always evident backstage. According to Mike, Tom was never 'pushing' to get a prime slot on any concert or television show.

Mike remembered that when he first started appearing at concerts and sharing the bill with other stars, there would be guys arguing over different slots on the shows.

'But Big Tom would be there with his whiskey in one hand, and back then when he smoked, a cigarette in the other. He'd just say, "Call me when you need me." That's how easy he was to work with,' remembered Mike.

Johnny McCauley, who wrote many of the greatest hits of Irish country music.

'Big Tom and The Mainliners were the biggest band ever in this country, whether you're into pop or rock, or if you're young or old. He's one of those names everyone knows,' he said, adding that he 'paved the pathway for all of us to do what we're doing now'.

Mike also said that Big Tom was somebody who all the stars that followed tried to emulate in different ways, 'but Tom had a unique voice, which really stood out from all others'.

He added that Tom was 'someone who was very relaxed. I suppose he didn't really want to be the centre of attention,' added Mike.

Big Tom was also a big influence on one of the newer country singers, Derek Ryan. He even shared the stage with Tom when he was a young boy.

'I got to support him when I was twelve years old. Myself and my brother supported Big Tom at the Lord Bagenal in Leighlinbridge, County Carlow.

'The band let me play the drums, and for weeks afterwards I told everybody I was playing Big Tom's drums – I was delighted with myself,' he added.

Speaking on Tipp FM radio with presenter Fran Curry, international singing star Tony Allen, of Foster & Allen fame, chart names from Westmeath to Wellington, New Zealand, paid tribute to Big Tom, along with his brother Tom (aka TR Dallas).

As the dancehall days in Ireland disappeared, TR had a big hit with a song about the demise of the dances, 'Big Tom Doesn't Play Here Anymore'. The song even had a Mainliners-sounding John Beattie-style organ solo, and some Seamus McMahon-sounding guitar licks towards the end.

The plaster is falling and the railings have come down
The dancers have moved away to another town
The stage that spoke so often is now an open door
Big Tom doesn't play here anymore.

'Big Tom Doesn't Play Here Anymore', TR Dallas (written by Tony Dunwoody)

The ballrooms became a relic of the past, as correctly and poignantly described in that song by TR, who continues to play on today. But everybody knows that Big Tom also played on, almost to the end of his days.

By that time, before and after he passed away, some critics in the media, who had lampooned and lambasted him in his earlier years, were lauding him. But one young new star in the media world who has been constructively supportive of Big Tom, and of country music in general, is RTÉ's 'Late Late Show' host Ryan Tubridy.

'It was an honour to be able to celebrate the life and impact of Big Tom on this year's Country Special, with some of his closest pals in the business,' he said. For two previous annual 'Late Late Show' Country Specials, Ryan had shown his respect for Big Tom and recognition for his contribution by having him on as a headline act.

'How are you, Tom?' asked Tubridy, when he first introduced him on the show, as he helped the slightly ailing Big Tom towards a high stool in the studio, while the audience gave him a standing ovation. With a glint of devilment in his eyes, Big Tom wittily, but certainly not wearily, replied: 'I'm fifty-one percent, and that's not bad for me!'

Two years later, Ryan was also at the helm as RTÉ screened the 'Late Late Show' special tribute to Big Tom, two days after he passed away. The TAM ratings showed that the tribute programme drew a fifty-one-percent (ironically that figure again!) share of the available television audience. The audience for the programme peaked at some 612,100 viewers, with the show having a reach of 1 million viewers who tuned in for some portion of the show across the night.

'One thing that we have learned from our specials is that the Irish country scene is really a family, and I want to thank everyone involved in the 2018 Country Special for allowing us to give Big Tom the send-off he very much deserved,' said the 'Late Late Show' host.

'With half the people watching television at the time tuned in, it is a testament to the popularity of the man and the music he loved so much,' added Ryan Tubridy. If Big Tom had been around, he would have made some wisecrack about 'too many people watching us on TV'.

As RTÉ producer Anne Roper wrote in the RTÉ Guide of 19 March 2006, in advance of her series, 'A Little Bit Country', Tom wasn't anxious to be in front of the cameras: 'Big Tom remains a gentle giant, who views fame with a healthy dose of humility.

Back then, thirteen years before he passed away, with all those tributes paid to him on television, on radio and in the press, and long before his massive final hit 'Going Out The Same Way You Came In', Tom predicted on 'A Little Bit Country' that, after a hiatus, country music in Ireland was enjoying a renaissance.

'Country music was big in the 'sixties; then disco started and pop bands, so country suffered,' he said. 'But recently, even just in the last year, there is a big swing back to country.

'There are lots of young people who want to see live bands, and there are an awful lot of young singers coming into country, bringing new people along,' said Tom in that 2006 television show.

In his interview with Anne Roper in the RTÉ Guide in March 2006, Tom added that once a person becomes a country fan, they remain one for life.

'Country music has always been different from other kinds of music. It's more traditional. If you make a fan, they'll follow and stay with you forever, thank God. They always have and always will.

'It's the music that draws us all together – songs with a story, and with a wee bit of a tear in them,' added Tom.

How right he was regarding fans staying with the country stars for life. The fans stayed, not just for life, but even after his life was over. The 9,000 or more that passed by his coffin, and the 2,000 that attended his burial, were living proof of how true Big Tom's words were all those years ago.

Strangely enough, while sections of the Dublin media derided the music of Big Tom, he had plenty of fans in Dublin too. It is interesting to note that two Letters to the Editor lionising Big Tom in the Sunday Independent of 22 April 2018, one of them adjudged as 'Letter of the Week', were both from fans with Dublin addresses.

The award-winning one was written by a Fred Molloy of Dublin 15, and was titled 'Ode to Big Tom':

Lie easy Big Tom McBride
You brought so much pride
To your county
And your country
A big man standing up on stage
Reaching out to all of each and every age.

The second letter was written by another Dublin resident – Margaret Walshe of Clonsilla, Dublin 15. It stated that 'Big Tom should have a State funeral'.

'Big Tom had a more positive impact on the mental and physical well-being, health, welfare and entertainment of more people, and over a much longer period, a lifetime, than most, and perhaps all Presidents and Taoisigh,' stated the letter.

But while that Dublin fan said that Tom should have a State funeral, in fact the funeral of the King of Irish Country was bigger that many Irish State funerals, according to a report in the *Irish World* newspaper, on 28 April 2018.

'It was the closest thing to a State funeral ever held in Ireland, as the country's most senior figures – and anyone who is anyone in Irish music – lined up to pay tribute to the King of Irish Country, Big Tom,' stated the opening lines of the report.

Meanwhile, in an interview on Radio Kerry, Mary Ryan, who was a resident singer in the Gresham Ballroom, Holloway Road, London in the 1960s, said Big Tom was 'by far the biggest attraction there. They absolutely adored him. Now, he was a young man back then, but he had signs of stardom at that time.

'There was a revolving stage there, and we would be playing for the first hour out front. Then the stage would revolve, and the visiting band would be there. But if you happened to fall getting off that revolving stage on the night Big Tom was there, they would absolutely trample on you to get as close as possible to the stage,' recalled Mary.

One of the tributes paid to Tom in this book comes from a person not in the media or in show business, and not a political, cultural or sporting leader either. This is his family GP, Dr Mary Flanagan. She recalls how Tom or Rose never looked for priority treatment.

'They came in to the surgery and stood in the queue; sometimes sat outside the surgery, waiting for it to open in the mornings. When they subsequently got inside, they took their places and sat with everybody else.

'I remember one morning in particular, when somebody, who was obviously a stranger in town, saw Big Tom outside the surgery. She followed him inside, and took a photograph of him as he was sitting in the queue. He thought it was so funny that at nine o'clock in the morning, somebody would find it interesting enough to take a picture of him,' says the doctor who attended to Rose and Tom for over twenty-five years.

'My experiences with Big Tom and Rose were always of two very nice, normal, accepting and down-to-earth people. In addition to that, they did not realise their position in our society, or in the national society,' says Dr Flanagan.

Minister of State and one of Tom's local TDs, Heather Humphreys was among those who extended sympathy to the family of the man known as the King of Country, according to the Anglo Celt newspaper:

'Big Tom was one of Monaghan's most famous sons and a true country music legend. His fantastic career spanned more than fifty years and, in June 2016, he was the first person ever inducted into Ireland's Country Music Hall of Fame.'

Minister Humphreys added: 'Big Tom was synonymous with Monaghan and he held a very special place in people's hearts in his native Oram and right across our county.

'It is fitting that the Carrickmacross–Castleblayney Municipal District are currently building a statue in Big Tom's honour. This will be a fitting tribute and there is absolutely no doubt that Big Tom's music and memory will live on forever,' she added.

As well as the politicians and the personalities, the ordinary fans, and friends, of Big Tom paid their respects and shared memories as they queued up in their thousands to file past his coffin, and later attend his burial.

One of these – John Pepper, a fan from childhood – probably summed up the feelings of many very well when interviewed for this book:

'Big Tom's music and songs touched the hearts of millions, not only in Ireland but across the globe, for more than half a century, spanning two millennia,' explained John.

'The stories and messages delivered by Big Tom, in his own inimitable style, had the hypnotic effect of allowing us to cast our minds back through the lens of nostalgia to our youth, when "the summers were always sunny"! To those romantic times of yesteryear, when we enjoyed a lifestyle not yet suffocated by world influences, with today's endless possibilities of instant gratification,' he added.

John alluded to the veneration that Irish people have in their hearts for their mothers, and how this was reflected in Big Tom's first hit.

'The precious place in our hearts that we Irish hold our mothers in, alive or departed, was touched on, not only by the lyrics of "Gentle Mother", but more especially by Big Tom's ability to give meaning to that song.

'It held a special place for him, as he frequently referenced the fact that "we all have a mother". The sentiment behind "Gentle Mother" may well have become a silent prayer for many of us,' added John.

This lifelong fan also stated that through his choice of songs, and his distinctive delivery, Big Tom relayed all that is at the heart of human relationships in their various dimensions.

'His various hits over the years touched on joy, sorrow, hurt, loss, tragedy and grief. He gave us a tremendous insight into his understanding of the journey of life; the value of good deeds ahead of earthly possessions; the importance of forgiveness; the worth of true friends; and faith in a better life in the next world,' added John.

Shades of songs that Big Tom sang, such as 'Far Side Banks Of Jordan' and 'Going Out The Same Way You Came In', are reflected in that statement.

Don't matter who you are,
Skid Row Joe or superstar,
You're going out the same way you came in.
'Going Out The Same Way You Came In', Big Tom (written by Max D Barnes)

That the music and the memory of Big Tom will live on, like that of Elvis Presley or Tom's idol Hank Williams, is a sentiment expressed in many tributes to Ireland's King of Country.

Writing in the *Western People* newspaper of 23 April 2018, after attending the funeral of Big Tom, Oliver Kelleher stated this succinctly:

'When Big Tom's name is mentioned in forty years' time, or his music played, people won't have to read Tom McBride on his CV. He will always be known as Big Tom, the King of Irish Country.'

Tom's long-time manager, musician and friend Kevin McCooey, speaking about his employer of over forty years, likened Tom's future memory to that of Elvis Presley, who we mentioned at the start of this chapter.

'There are two photographs of Elvis Presley currently on the wall and window of one of the hairdressers here in town [Castleblayney], and he's dead for fifty years. But his memory lives on, and his music is still being played and sounds as fresh as ever. So also will the songs of Big Tom, such as "Four Country Roads", still be played and be part of Irish culture a half a century from now,' said Kevin.

It seems we'll have to contradict to the title of the TR Dallas hit, mentioned earlier in this chapter, 'Big Tom Doesn't Play Here Anymore'. It seems that, like Hank or Elvis, Big Tom's songs may be played here for evermore, be it in Ireland, or wherever Irish emigrants gather for a sing-song.

'Four Country Roads (to Glenamaddy)' will frequently be sung alongside other iconic Irish songs, such as 'The Fields Of Athenry', 'Dublin In The Rare Auld Times', 'The N17', 'Lovely Leitrim', 'My Donegal Shore' or 'Whiskey In The Jar'.

In his passing, Big Tom, Ireland's country music monarch, was remembered and revered across all strands of society, from the President of the nation to the fans in the street, the farm, the factory, the office, the home and everywhere else.

Chapter 12

Not Going Out the Same Way He Came In!

F rom the four corners of Ireland and from overseas too, they came for the funeral of a King, the King of Country in Ireland, Big Tom.

They travelled along many country roads, from every direction, and not just from Glenamaddy. But then Big Tom's 'Four Country Roads' could refer to anywhere in Ireland, from Kerry to Derry, from Down or Antrim to Kildare. if we deviate from the original lyrics:

Four roads to Ballykelly
Four roads that drift apart
Four roads to Ballykelly
Are the four dusty byways to my heart.

There's a Ballykelly in Derry, Down, Antrim and Kildare, and there are four roads to and from almost every little town and village in Ireland.

One can complete a tour of the four provinces of Ireland by linking villages of the same name in counties Galway and Kerry, as follows:

Four roads to Kilconly
Four roads that drift apart
Four roads to Kilconly
Are the four dusty byways to my heart.

It could be 'Four Roads To Castleblayney', or you can write your own lyrics linking 'Four Country Roads' to a town or village near you. That's a tribute to how relevant the song is to anywhere in Ireland.

But travelling from the west to and from Castleblayney, the country roads are long and winding. Sometimes the route gets narrow, almost like any of the four roads to Glenamaddy. You pass by high hedges, lakes and wetlands, alongside the little hills of Monaghan, coming from Cavan, Leitrim, Longford or wherever.

The fans, friends and many high-profile personalities travelled those roads, and along other routes for Tom's funeral. But one can only envisage how it might have been for the singer and his musicians in the past, traversing those dusty, long and winding roads, often six nights a week. This is the tough side of working for a living in what many see as the glamorous world of show business.

The dawn would be breaking on many a wet morning, and on many a morning the little hills and roads might look beautiful clad in a blanket of white snow, glistening with a covering of hard frost and ice. Then driving could be treacherous. During all these years of travelling, there must have been times when those musicians would have preferred to be covered in a blanket and warm in their beds. But instead, they were out in the middle of the night, navigating one of the shining, slippery roads back to Castleblayney through a winter wonderland.

Perhaps during times like this, Tom's song 'It's A Weary Weary World' might have resonated with him, and the musicians, as they made yet another journey along the four, or more, dangerously wet, windswept, winding roads, maybe from Glenamaddy in the west, back to 'Blayney.

But the sun shone brightly during the days of Big Tom's funeral and burial, as mourners by the thousands travelled to and from his home village to say their farewells. It was shining brightly too, through the front window of his home a few years earlier, on a warm Saturday evening, as we chatted about how the increasing amount of traffic on the rural roads made travelling to and from gigs more tiresome for musicians.

'I don't travel as much anymore, as the amount of traffic on the roads has got so great in the last few years. It was very small when we started out. You could plan the time it would take to go to Galway or Mayo or Cork from Castleblayney. Back then, you'd know you would be there in that amount of time.

'But now you haven't an idea. You'd almost need to leave home the day before to get there in time,' said Tom with a laugh.

Of course, there were great times too for Tom, even when he wasn't travelling as much. There was the time the fans travelled to 'Blayney when a bronze plaque of him was unveiled at the Oram GAA Centre. But Tom said that when he found out about it, he was 'ready to kill those who came up with such an idea'.

Later on, five years before his passing, Tom and fellow entertainers Paddy Cole and Anna McGoldrick were accorded the Freedom of Castleblayney, and many fans travelled to witness the event.

When Mayor Garry Carville said that he was calling on Big Tom to say a few words, it was the witty side of Tom that was first to emerge in his short speech.

'If I know Tom, the words will be very few,' he said, as the crowd roared with laughter. He added that he was thanking everyone on behalf of the band and himself, and added: 'It's lovely to get the freedom of a town, especially when it's your home town.'

Gracious as ever in his praise for others, Tom congratulated the other recipients of the freedom of the town, Paddy Cole and Anna McGoldrick. He also thanked his late friend Johnny McCauley for writing 'Back to Castleblayney' and so many other songs for him.

Perhaps such events rejuvenated Tom. Certainly, his love of performing, and of meeting so many of the fans after gigs, saw him go back on the road again and again, for tour after tour, even when his health was failing, and right up until a few months before he passed away.

On 30 August 2018, he performed at his last television concert, for TG4's 'Opry Dhoire' in Derry's Millennium Forum. Even then, though obviously ailing, and sitting on a high chair while singing, he still sounded as good as ever. He was not devoid either of making humorous utterances, even in the middle of the song 'You Are My Sunshine'. Tom deviated from the lyrics to put in some of his own:

You are my sunshine
My packet of Woodbine
My bottle of whiskey
That makes me frisky.

The adoring crowd reacted to his new lyrics in this old country classic by laughing, cheering and clapping along.

The fans, and his fellow performers, returned all the good humour, love and affection that he always had for them by ensuring that all the country roads, to and from 'Blayney, were chock-a-block with traffic for his final farewell.

In the church in Oram, his grandchildren brought memorabilia of his career and his life to the altar. All sorts of songs, from gospel to country and traditional to bluegrass, were sung. Father Leo Creelman said it was a heartbreaking replay of events for the McBride family, less than eighty days after the passing of their mother, grandmother and Tom's 'devoted and beloved wife Rose'.

'Tom and Rose were a partnership that worked, an example of where each spouse cared for the other more than themselves.

'A glimmer of comfort is perhaps that God was merciful in allowing Tom to be united so quickly again with his beloved Rose.'

Mourners were told how Tom and Rose had been married for fifty-two years, and their children were accustomed to a house full of people – a place where the kettle was never off the boil, and friends and neighbours were always welcomed inside.

But there was humour in his eulogy too, just as Big Tom would have liked. Father Leo recounted the dry wit of the singer, which he delivered in his own inimitable way.

He said: 'The family told me that Rose was once getting dressed up in her finest – a dress rehearsal for an upcoming wedding.

'As she appeared in the kitchen and asked for an opinion, resplendent in a beautiful hat with feathers on top, Tom piped up, "It's a terror what you see when you haven't got your gun with you!"' (Irish Sun, 20 April)

'Despite all his success and fame, he always remained humble and down to earth, and first and foremost a family man.

'He was a man big in stature, matched up with an even bigger heart,' added Father Creelman.

Everyone at that funeral Mass, earlier at the wake, and afterwards at the burial, had their own special memories of Big Tom. People spoke mostly of happy times, when his songs and music were uplifting interludes in their lives.

But there were some fans too who had memories of how Tom, and Rose, helped them through darker times of tragedy. These included Padraic and Mary O'Hehir from the Mayo–Galway border village of Clonbur, who sadly lost a son in a jet skiing tragedy.

'Rose rang us regularly, and when I was in hospital one time, they couldn't do enough for us, and were ringing Mary to make sure that we were alright,' said Padraic. The couple were in Oram for both Tom's and Rose's funerals and burials.

'They were genuine, caring, sincere people, and they meant what they said.

'Last summer, my family had a surprise sixtieth birthday party for me in Clonbur, and in the middle of the party there was a phone call from Rose and Tom. They would have given anything to be at the party, but at the time he wasn't well enough for travelling,' said Padraic.

He added that it is 'so tough on the children and grandchildren that they have lost both their parents within such a short time of each other.'

Padraic added that, from dealing with tragedy in his own family, his advice is to always continue talking about their great memories of Tom and Rose.

'We have always continued talking about our son Patrick, who sadly lost his life at the age of twenty-two, when he was on a jet ski on a Mayo lake over eleven years ago.'

Singing star Brian Coll, a contemporary of Big Tom's during the dance-hall days, was among those who sang at his graveside. He also talked about Tom's caring nature when he was in hospital twenty-nine years earlier, after suffering a brain haemorrhage.

Tom reassured him that he would recover, saying: 'We will not be going on tour and not be meeting Brian Coll. That wouldn't be right.'

When Tom died, Brian had 'twenty phone calls' telling him the sad news, 'including two from New York', he told Nicola Anderson in the Irish Independent of Saturday, 21 April 2018.

Tom had that same caring attitude for stars such as Brian Coll as he had for his fans and for the tramp on the street, about whom he recorded a song, by one of his idols, Hank Williams.

'Not only did Big Tom sing about "The Tramp On The Street", he prac-tised what he sang,' says his long-time friend and fan John Pepper.

'In an article in one of the Sunday newspapers after his death, a jour-nalist relayed a story about when working, several years ago in London, he witnessed Big Tom stopping to speak with a poor man sitting begging on the street, on a Sunday morning. The journalist remarked on the time Big Tom spent talking to the man, and he then handed him £50, before heading on about his business.'

That was indicative of Big Tom's generosity to everyone, including to that tramp on a London street.

He was some mother's darlin', he was some mother's son
Once he was fair and once he was young.

'Tramp On The Street', Hank Williams (written by Grady and Hazel Cole)

Big Tom was never one to be critical of other people, or of how they might have slipped down the ladder in life. Perhaps he lived his life by the words of the monologue, 'Be Careful Of Stones That You Throw'.

In the words of that monologue, one of the few that Big Tom ever recorded, he uses the spoken word, as well as singing, to earnestly tell the listener that unless he/she 'has made no mistakes' in life, they should 'be careful of stones that [they] throw'.

This monologue had previously been recorded by two of Tom's idols, Hank Williams and Porter Wagoner. Tom also recorded Wagoner's 'Old Log Cabin For Sale', and it became his second big hit. He was influenced to record it by the version that he heard earlier by Porter.

'He had a sort of sadness in his voice that I liked, and I recorded about half-a-dozen of his songs.

'The record "Old Log Cabin for Sale" was the first Porter Wagoner song that I recorded. It had another great song on the "B" side – "If You're Lonesome At Your Table",' said Tom in our 2004 interview.

There were funny memories also related at the funeral, and afterwards. These included one published the following Sunday by Eddie Rowley in the Sunday World. This was about an alleged incident in London involving Big Tom and another of his contemporaries from the showband days – the late, great Joe Dolan.

'It happened in The Galtymore,' Tom confirmed to Eddie. 'There were two halls, and I was in one and Joe in the other.

'After the dance, I went up to the bar, and I heard a voice singing behind me, "four country roads".

'I didn't have to turn around. I knew who it was. I just said, "it's you, it's you, it's you". Then you could hear that great laugh that Joe had. Ah, we had great craic,' added Tom.

While their styles of songs were different, Big Tom and Joe Dolan, as well as Larry Cunningham, all came from the showband era of the 1960s, and all continued recording and playing almost up to the end of their days.

While Joe's songs were mostly in the pop genre, both Tom and Larry sang songs that were either country or Irish. Some of these were about places in Ireland that the Irish diaspora in the UK identified with.

Sometimes these songs were written by Irish exiles, such as Johnny McCauley in London, who wrote most of Big Tom's songs. Another exile was Kevin Kelly, who wrote 'Connemara Shore' for Tom.

'He lived in Birmingham, and he came up to me one night and gave me a demo tape of the song. He said it might be suitable for me to record.

'The song was "Connemara Shore", and I loved it as soon as I heard it. It was a mighty song, and it didn't take me long to get it down on record,' said Tom in the 2004 interview.

'It was a hugely popular song for us, and while you might expect songs like that to be popular in the place that was mentioned in them, such as in Connemara or in Galway, that one was popular everywhere.

'It's like "Four Country Roads", which was as popular in Donegal as it would be in Galway or Glenamaddy. Another example was "Back to Castleblayney", which was as popular among the Irish in England as it was in Castleblayney. Songs that become hits don't just become hits in the one area,' he added.

Of course he was correct in this observation, as songs such as 'The Streets Of London' or 'Galveston' or 'The Fields Of Athenry', to name but three examples, have been hits with people in countries thousands of miles away from the places mentioned in the songs.

In that same interview with Big Tom, he said that while he loved what he did in life, he had some words of warning for his grandchildren, or for any young person contemplating a career on the music scene.

'You need to have dedication, because it can be hard work, if you're living out of a suitcase every night.

'Also you need to get the right breaks, and the right material to record. If the people like what you are doing, you are made. But if not, then you can forget about it,' were his cautionary words.

Tom had many highs in his career. He sold over 100,000 copies of the Ashes of Love album in 1972–73. He played to 82,000 fans at the London–Irish Festival in 1979. He recorded in Nashville the following year, and achieved 1 million album sales in that year also.

Another highlight was having the biggest-selling single in Ireland in 1981, with 'Four Country Roads'. Yet another was going back on the road in the 1990s with the original Mainliners, and their sporadic but sold-out tours in the 2000s. In this new millennium too, he had one of the biggest hits of his long career with 'Going Out The Same Way You Came In'.

But Big Tom came across, at all times that I've met him over the decades, as a contented man, so humble that he would never boast about any of the highlights of his storied career. He was contented with his lot in life, a contented family man, and rightly so. He was contented too with the songs that he recorded. But he was also a realist. Even when questioned about death, Tom wasn't afraid to say, in an interview in 2017, that it might not be far away.

'How would you describe your life now?' asked Mary Kennedy in that interview, for RTÉ's 'Nationwide' programme.

Without blinking an eye, Tom replied. 'Coming to an end, but I'm still enjoying what I'm doing.'

'Hopefully I'll enjoy it for another while. You can't go on forever, but I hope to enjoy it for as long as I can,' he added.

Maybe these lines from a song titled 'There's A Time', recorded for one of his last albums, also hint at what he might have been thinking about his own mortality:

> *Time changes everything*
> *Nothing stays the same*
> *And the further down the road you get*
> *The less you feel the pain*
> *There's a time to hurt and a time to heal*
> *There's a time for movin' on*
> *And everyone in life deserves*
> *Their time, out in the sun.*
>
> Big Tom (written by Eugene Cunningham)

Perhaps death did not hold too much fear for Big Tom, as he had enjoyed his time out in the sun. To quote words from William Shakespeare's Julius Caesar, written back in 1599:

> *Cowards die many times before their deaths;*
> *The valiant never taste death but once.*
> *Of all the wonders that I yet have heard,*
> *It seems to me most strange that men should fear;*

Seeing that death, a necessary end,
Will come when it will come.

Julius Caesar, Act II, Scene 2

Big Tom, as stated elsewhere, was seen by many in the mould of another of his idols, Merle Haggard, a poet of the common man. While his fans hoped he could go on forever, he had various serious health issues to deal with in his final years.

Big Tom came through all those health issues quietly, but he was realistic and conscious of his own mortality. Tom wasn't afraid to talk about, or sing about, the reality that we're going out the same way we came in, to borrow words from his big hit.

You may drive a Coupe de Ville,
Own a mansion on the hill,
Don't mean nothing when St Peter calls your name.

Big Tom (written by Max D Barnes)

Tom had given his all to the music he loved, to the fans he loved and to the friends he loved, but most of all to the family he loved.

Perhaps that is why his funeral, and burial, were a celebration of a life well lived. A celebration full of music and song and dance, for a man who had ensured that people enjoyed music, song and dance, all during his long career.

Everybody there in Oram during those days knew; everybody watching on television knew; as did those listening on radio, reading about the obsequies in the newspapers, or on social media; that Tom's musical legacy will live on. Death did not stop people dancing to the music and the songs of Big Tom, even in the cemetery, as his friends sang his songs and played his music.

The scene on a previous evening too, when his remains lay in repose in the local GAA Centre, was captured succinctly in words by Oliver Kelleher in the Western People:

'The mood outside the clubhouse was a happy one. People young and old turned up, chatting about the man as if he was just about to go on stage.'

At the graveside too, stars from the music scene lined up to sing songs in honour of Big Tom, in what the Irish Independent headlined as a 'Rollicking Tribute to the King of Irish Country'.

Of course, his friend Susan McCann was there, to sing a verse of her number one hit, the song that immortalised Tom decades earlier, 'Big Tom Is Still The King'. Other veterans singing in the sunshine in the cemetery included his old friend Margo, who had recorded that final duet hit with him, 'A Love That's Lasted Through The Years', only months earlier. Sandy Kelly was there of course, who also recorded a Top Ten hit with Tom – 'You Needed Me', back in 1984. Years later, she had had another number one duet hit with 'The Woodcarver', with another country icon, now sadly deceased too – Johnny Cash.

And the youngsters were there also. Among those to come forward and sing was seventeen-year-old Keelan, who hit all the right notes on the gospel classic 'I Saw The Light'. He has since recorded 'When Big Tom Sang Gentle Mother', co-written by Margo, who first introduced the youngster to Tom.

'Big Tom was such a gentleman to talk to, and he gave me great advice about the music business. I have been a fan of his songs for years, and am honoured and humbled to sing at his graveside, and to record a tribute song about him,' Keelan added.

Another young singer at the graveside was Barry McAllister, seventeen, from Donaghmoyne in County Monaghan, who said that Big Tom was his first musical inspiration.

'I currently play myself and gig in local venues, so I suppose without him, I mightn't have.

'But look, he's a cultural icon – a son of Ireland and a son of Monaghan. A real hero figure,' stated Barry in an *Irish Daily Mail* interview in April 2018.

Tom was also a cultural icon in the minds of the members of Claremorris Municipal District in Mayo, who passed a vote of sympathy to the McBride family.

It was proposed by Councillor Gerry Murray, who said, 'Big Tom was a cultural icon who had an amazing impact on the lives of so many people,' according to the *Mayo News*.

The national media were there in force too, to report on his funeral Mass and burial. Many stories and photographs have been published since, of what was an enormous celebration of Big Tom's life. It was covered in depth on television, in the press – regional, national and international – as well as on social media. Shannonside–Northern Sound radio also broadcast the funeral Mass.

The *Irish Independent* reported that 'the most devoted of his fans, who were now old friends, were there, recognising each other's faces from his concerts down the years.

'We'll never see each other again now,' said Patricia Courtney, from Julianstown in County Meath, who followed him for forty-seven years, since she was seventeen years old.'

Prior to the funeral, one of the religious leaders to express his sadness at the passing of Big Tom was Monsignor Joseph McGuinness, from the Diocese of Clogher, where Tom lived.

'Like many people around the country, we have all learned with great sadness of the death of Big Tom. The word "legend" is often overused on occasions like this, but in Tom's case it is truly fitting and well deserved. During his life, Tom brought great joy to many people, both in Ireland and worldwide, through his singing and his music. His contribution to Irish social and cultural life in this area has been enormous.

'But Tom McBride was more than just a singer. Above all, he was a family man. Tom, and his late wife Rose, formed a strong team in their household and in the wider community. Tom was a pivotal member of the community in his native Oram, where he contributed greatly through farming and sport. He was very proud of that community, and of County Monaghan in general'.

Henry McMahon, band leader with the Mainliners, and Kevin McCooey, long time manager of Big Tom and former musician in his band The Travellers, at Tom's funeral.

As his remains reposed in his beloved Oram GAA Centre, players and friends from the football club formed a guard of honour. They performed the same duty when the hearse took his coffin on his last road journey. Later, at his funeral Mass and in the cemetery, the community of County Monaghan and the people of Ireland gave Big Tom the sort of send-off that would be fit for the King of a country – after all, he was the King of Country.

Father Creelman's homily at the Mass, and Jim O'Neill's eulogy at the graveside, have been well documented elsewhere in the media. But one month later, when the more private Month's Mind Mass was celebrated in Oram church, without the glare of the media, the church was still filled to overflowing.

At that Mass, the celebrant, Father Vincent Sherlock, remarked that this massive crowd, both inside and outside the church, was testament to how popular and loved Big Tom was.

'If there was ever any doubt in the family's minds – and there is no reason to think they ever had – of the difference he made in the lives of so many people, all they need do is look around at all that are here again today,' said Father Sherlock.

'The people have filled this church again, not because of cameras, news or media. They have travelled to be here today to remember your father, your grandfather, your brother, your friend, your neighbour from here in Oram,' said Tom's friend Jim O'Neill.

He continued: 'I think that, as referenced in a poem read earlier at this Mass, there is "a quiet Ireland", and this is it. This is Ireland at its very best; people have a tune in their heads and in their hearts, and a memory for a man who made a difference.'

Also at that Month's Mind Mass, Margo sang her song ending in the words: 'Their paths have been trod, Rose and Tom are home with God.' She also led the congregation in the gospel song 'Never Grow Old'.

Tom and Rose's neighbour Jim O'Neill, in his eulogy, read a poem sent in the post by a man from Donegal. He had seen a woman, a fan of Big Tom's, get on a bus in Omagh, and it was evident that she was distressed at the passing of her idol.

'She was weepy and sad, and just could not stop talking about Big Tom and her love for dancing, her life-long memories, Tom's music and his songs.

'This lady carried two red roses, and she told all on the bus that she was on her way to Oram to attend Tom's wake. One rose was for Tom, and the other for his dear wife Rose,' said Jim.

He added that the man, a passenger on the bus, was greatly moved, and wrote the poem about his experience.

'This unknown woman's unashamed outpouring of grief mirrored exactly what we ourselves all felt. It also highlighted the massive impact and the everlasting impression that Big Tom had on all our lives.'

'Two Roses for Big Tom' by Tommie Francis

She got on the bus in Omagh
The town that she was from
To go to Castleblayney
With two roses for Big Tom.
A rose for all the memories
For all the joy and love
And a rose for Rose in Heaven
Who was waiting up above.

Although I'd never seen her
And I didn't know her name
There was something that I saw in her
That made her seem the same
As every gentle mother
With her sorrow and her tears
And every girl from Omagh
Who had danced down through the years.

Who had followed in Tom's footsteps
In each hall and marquee
She collected all his records
Every tape and DVD
From the roads to Glenamaddy
And other journeys he would make
Now she went to Castleblayney
With two roses for his wake.

She had danced her way through Ireland
From Cork to Donegal
If you couldn't dance to Big Tom
Then you couldn't dance at all.
But every dance comes to an end
And gentle hearts will break
So she went to Castleblayney
With red roses for his wake.

As I watched her getting off that bus
I knew she was part
Of the quiet soul of Ireland
Where his music stirred the heart
And the music is still living
And I hoped it healed her ache
As she walked through Castleblayney
With two roses for his wake.

I saw her with the roses
As she drifted through the street
In the comfort and the company
Of everyone she'd meet
And I knew romantic Ireland
Will not be dead and gone
It will dance and live forever
In the music of Big Tom.

Big Tom was a private and shy star, but he was always available to his fans to chat after his dances, or if they called around to see him at home. Is it any wonder then that on the first day of his wake, over 9,000 mourners filed past his coffin in Oram Community Centre?

'It was apt that Tom McBride had a public wake, because his whole life was an open book.

'And what a life of achievements there were to recall, for those who came to bid goodbye to Tom at Oram Community Centre in County Monaghan,' stated John Fitzgerald, writing in Ireland's Eye magazine in June 2018. He added that he first 'had the good fortune' to meet Tom when he performed at a Carnival dance in Callan, County Kilkenny, in the mid-1970s.

'He struck me as a humble person, not remotely conscious of his fame or popularity. That accords very much with the general impression of the man, as attested to by the multiple lavish tributes that followed in the days following his departure from this world,' stated the *Ireland's Eye* story.

His iconic status will always be clear when people view the statue in his memory in his home town of Castleblayney. Not that Tom ever wanted any statues or plaques of him erected anywhere. Indeed, when told that he would have to model for the statue, his reply was a humorous one.

'I hope they don't want me to take too much off,' quipped Tom with a grin.

The statue, erected by the local Municipal District Council, is something Tom never lived to see. Another project, suggested by his former manager Robert Irwin, is for the Market House in Castleblayney to be restored and refurbished as a museum, for displaying memorabilia on all forms of Irish music. There would be a section for the music and memorabilia of Big Tom, the singer who never retired.

Retirement wasn't a word that appeared in Tom's vocabulary. When asked about it, even a few months before he passed away, as usual the big man had a very witty reply.

'Retirement? What's that?' Tom said to Mary Kennedy when she asked him if he had any plans to hang up his guitar.

'Retirement? Oh! I don't know about that, but for a living I don't think there is anything that I could have liked better than music, and the music has been very, very good to me,' concluded Big Tom.

This humble farmer, hayshed-erecter, pipe-layer, tomato-picker and ice cream-maker had, in his life, become a music hit-maker supreme.

To paraphrase his own last hit, Big Tom wasn't going out the same way he came in!

As Shane McGowan, and so many others, rightly said, and as Susan McCann sang, 'Big Tom Is Still The King' of Irish country.

'Big Tom Is Still The King' Susan McCann
(song lyrics adapted by Michael Commins)

The ballrooms in this country are living proof today
Of a man who's now a legend from Wicklow to Galway
We love our country music, to us it's everything
It don't matter what they tell you, Big Tom is still the King.

With fever-pitched excitement, country music on our mind
I'd drive one hundred miles to hear that voice so warm and kind
And I can still recall now the first time I heard him sing
I feel proud to be from 'Blayney, where Big Tom is still the King.

You can have your Waylon Jennings or Nashville's Charlie Pride
They boast of all their superstars, but for us it's Tom McBride
Oh Nashville is so far away, it scarcely means a thing
But when you're in Old Ireland, Big Tom is still the King.

Next time you're down in Wexford or West in old Mayo
Don't need to ask who's the King? They chose Big Tom long ago
You can ask the stars in Ireland, they say he's got the swing
They'd be the first to tell you, Big Tom is still the King

'The Legend Of Big Tom' (by PJ Murrihy)

He had a gentle mother

And he was a gentle son

Our voice of country music

He was loved by everyone

Tom McBride from Oram

Near Castleblayney town

A part of us went with you

The day we laid you down

Uneasy he wore the crown

As Ireland's country king

Said goodbye and then went out

The same way he came in

The blue and white of Monaghan

Was Tom's great pride and joy

He wore them on the field of play

Back when he was a boy

He must have sung a thousand songs

And shook a million hands

Brought Ireland to our exiles

Far from their native land

He lost the strength to carry on

When his Rose did depart

And to join her seemed the only way

To mend his broken heart

The great man will be honoured
As the Irish hearts lament
But Tom McBride's good name
Will be his greatest monument

Their grieving family can walk tall
And hold their heads up high
And be proud to have such parents
As Big Tom and Rose McBride.

Acknowledgements

Tom Gilmore thanks the McBride family for their support, co-operation, interviews and the contribution of so much research material, photographs, scrapbooks, etc., for this book. Thanks also to Paddy King and Madge McBride-Kavanagh. Particular thanks to Margo O'Donnell, whose help in putting this project together was invaluable.

Thanks also to Big Tom's many colleagues in the music business – singers, songwriters, musicians, managers and record company personnel – and, of course, the late Rose McBride. To Tom's neighbours, fans and friends, who all gave their time and their memories freely to me in interviews for this book.

My gratitude also to the President of Ireland, Michael D. Higgins, for so graciously giving me permission to reproduce the text of his heartfelt tribute to Big Tom.

I would also like to mention Ann, Raymond, Louise and Matthew Quirke, who have always been there for me when often needed over the years. To the extended Collins family in Chester, for their love and inspiration, and in particular Richard Collins and Melissa Shaw, for vital social media research for this book.

Thanks also to my 'other family' and friends in Perth, Western Australia, and to Sean Burke, Milltown and Tuam, for his indispensable audio and video expertise for this project. Also to Father Brian D'Arcy, Michael Commins, Dennis Heaney, Susan McCann and Steve Brink, for advice and help.

My gratitude to the extended Gilmore families in counties Galway, Cork and Sligo, and to all others who encouraged this project, especially David Burke, Editor, and my colleagues in the *Tuam Herald*. Also my colleagues in Galway Bay FM, and in particular Dylan Connolly, John Mulligan and David Nevin, for their technical talents in transferring interviews from older audio formats to new technology, and to Sean Walsh of Trad Ireland Recordings, Renmore. And to Owen Breslin for invaluable help with sourcing photographs.

To the publishers, O'Brien Press, in particular Michael O'Brien and editor Eoin O'Brien, for their unwavering support for this project. Also to Ruth Heneghan and Geraldine Feehily, for their endless encouragement and enthusiasm.

Thanks to RTÉ and the many other media outlets, TV, broadcast and print media, whose interviews, reports and photographic coverage of Big Tom's career are referred to in the pages of this book. Apologies if I've inadvertently omitted anyone.

Above all else, thanks to Big Tom for the magical musical memories. His songs will last forever – truly The King of Irish Country Music.

Other books from the O'Brien Press

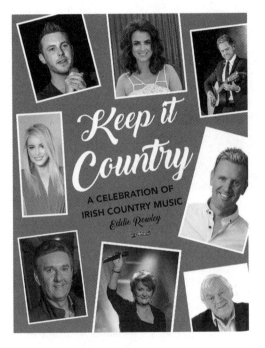

The stars. The legends. The passion.

From Big Tom, Philomena and Daniel to Nathan, Lisa, Mike and many more, the leading lights of Irish country in their own words. Discover what inspired their drive for stardom and a life on the road. A treasure trove of exclusive interviews and photographs.

Hardback ISBN: 978-1-84717-968-5

Philomena Begley takes us from her happy beginnings as a breadman's daughter in Pomeroy through the devastating loss of her brother Patsy and the risks of touring Ireland at the height of the Troubles, right up to her fiftieth anniversary in show business in 2012 – her 'gold and silver days'.

Hardback ISBN: 978-1-84717-966-1

In Ireland, Daniel O'Donnell is more than just a singing star: he has reached the status of 'national treasure'. It has been a long journey for the boy from Kincasslagh, County Donegal, and in this updated autobiography, he tells his story with his customary sense of humour and down-to-earth charm.

Hardback ISBN: 978-1-84717-967-8

DANIEL O'DONNELL

Living the Dream

The official memoir of Margo O'Donnell, legendary Irish country music singer. For fifty years now the name 'Margo' has been synonymous with everything that is positive and enriching in Irish country music. This is the story of her life, the successes and difficult times, in her own words.

Hardback ISBN: 978-1-84717-674-5

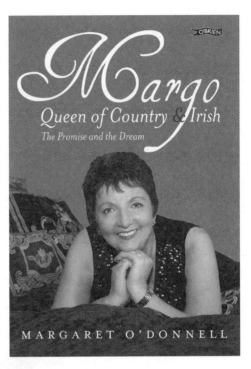

Read the story of Joe Dolan through his own interviews and the memories and anecdotes of his family that vividly bring to life the essence of Joe.

Paperback ISBN: 978-1-84717-219-8